The Phoenix Living Poets

JOURI

JOURNEY
INTO MORNING

By

D. J. HALL

CHATTO AND WINDUS

THE HOGARTH PRESS

1972

Published by
Chatto & Windus Ltd
40/42 William IV Street
London W.C.2

ISBN 0 7011 1795 8

Distributed in the United States of America
by Wesleyan University Press

ISBN 0 8195 7040 0

Printed in Great Britain by
Lewis Reprints Limited
London and Tonbridge

CONTENTS

For
ISABEL

PROLOGUE

Humbly I beg the goddess help my theme:
If out-of-date such modesty may seem
It is not only customary but wise,
Remembering Thamyris lost both his eyes,
His skill in harping and his gift of song,
Because the Muses naturally found wrong
His boasting that his music rivalled theirs:
Such peacock-pride was bound to end in tears.

Now, as we sail on dark yet charted seas,
My theme contains what magic you may please
To give it, since the work of poetry
Is so to dominate reality,
That, when its magic plays a fantasy
Fulfilment of a truth you wish could be,
You, yourself, make it true since made to act
As though already it were so in fact.

This is the quiddity of poetry,
To strive that the impossible may be
And so sometimes achieve it. The world then
Stays objectively the same? But when
Our view of it is changed it changes too;
So are our lives transformed by a cuckoo
That turns our winter into spring, making
A new vision between sleep and waking.

Since everyone may have this vision,
The poet sheds freely through elision
Some of his individuality
To share a world of sensibility

That all experience. This world, the Muse
Helping me, is my aim; and I shall use
All tricks of metre that she may advance
To lull yet make it still a lively trance.

Fish-pink Venetian silhouette
Glows in the Gothic-Byzantine sunset:
Fitting it is to leave from this city
Wedded to the sea where intensity
Of sun marries moon-dark each ship that plies
Sails into an Ionian sunrise.
We sail as all do each with his own quest,
Mine is Apollo's 'Know thyself!'. How best
Can we learn? We'll thresh out the Cyclades.
Begin then, goddess, at what point you please.

I

Genesis - The voyage begins - Ithacan dawn - Callisto
and the professors emerge - Delphi - 'too much, too soon'.

In the beginning was breathless nothingness:
Darkness and brightness, here there or anywhere,
Had no place in uncreated nowhere.

Into the nothing came naked Eurynome
Dancing and dancing with nothing to dance upon,
Further and further dividing the nothing
Till up swept a sky and away fell a sea:
Lonely Eurynome, Goddess of All Things,
Seeing nothing but sensing a pursuer,
Screamed with no sound in the sundered chaos,
Fled on the foam in the still blind void
Till rounding in rage she wrestled with the tramontane,
Writhing as she pummelled it between her palms,
Feeling it shape a serpent out of nothingness:
Suddenly cold in the gusty emptiness,
She danced in her last invisible wildness
Fanning the flame of her virgin nakedness,
Sharpening the serpent-northwind's lust.

Ophion-Boreas coiled and coupled with her.

Transformed to a dove, Eurynome drifted
Then dived to settle her breast on the waves,
Rocking restless with beak tucked warmly,
She brooded for millenniums upon the Egg:
Then what was timeless suddenly was instant,

Eurynome called on Ophion-Boreas
To encoil seven times this round reality.
A first sound shattered the primaeval silence:
The hair-line crack of the splitting egg.

Laughing Eurynome, casting her feathers,
Counted her children, then, filling the firmament,
Fearfully first loosed the pale Moon-Mother;
Sun, stars, mountains, rivers gouging,
Beast, birds, fish and all things growing,
All that breathed except man's likeness
Moved from emptiness into brightness,
Searching the earth's most suitable places,
Tearing the silence with tumult of voices.

Eurynome then with Ophion following
Went to Olympus, but, when as her consort
He boasted too loudly of fathering Creation,
She kicked out his teeth and banished him below:
So there dwelt the python with heel-bruised head,
While his twin-self, Boreas, freely blew,
A sanctus spiritus fertilising mares.
But the serpent's teeth combined with the dust,
And when a mist went up and watered them
Mankind sprouted with breath and a soul:
At that time were created the Titans,
Parents and foes of the Gods, their children,
Who fought them for ten years led by Zeus,
Hera, his sister-wife, and Poseidon . . .

   'Poseidon,' said professor Tarragon, 'had brought
                            Odysseus to this pass.'
I watch the red ball burning Ithaca's black ridge
Suffuse the dawn sky, while the fluttered sea stays wine-dark
As a filled goblet gazed into not held against the light,
And the ship's deck warms as the shadows shorten.

'See the cleft,' he says, 'that runs up from the water's edge?
There, in a cave, Odysseus hid on his return
The gifts of cauldrons and the gold of Alcinous,
And there divine Athene came to him disguised
As a young shepherd, beautiful with white sandalled
                                        feet and javelin
Claiming Zeus as father, she denied Poseidon,
The earth-shaker god of sea and horses,
Whom some said sired her and whose tantrums
Drove her to succour sufferers from his spite.
Now with Odysseus she hatched a scheme
To slay the suitors of his wife, Penelope,
Who thought him dead. Look you, there
Where a long-leaved olive grows above the cave
That has one mouth for men, another for the gods;
Within were jars which bees used for their hives
And looms of stone where Naiads wove sea-purple;
There, in that cave, some forty years ago were found
The hidden cauldrons that Odysseus brought home -
There! Below the sun's eye, do you see?
Phocys, Old Man of the Sea, named the bay,
Though he lies lazily in Egypt with his seals.'

Professor Tarragon smiles vaguely at the dawn,
As though a puzzling thought has come to him
That this dawn, though like many he has seen,
Is heralding no ordinary consequence:
The light breeze ruffles through his long, fair hair,
His searching, blue eyes see beyond the shore;
His listeners, by his abstraction awed,
Assume the mien of knowing reverence
They feel required of them on sight of Greece:
At length, when it is clear he has forgotten them,
They go below to finish getting drest,
Bearing a nimbus air of being blest.

5

Those cauldrons, a short swim across the strait!
I stay with silence at my side: my love,
With eyes closed to the glare and wax-smooth face,
Is like a kore with archaically
Amused, curved mouth, cheeks high and round as pithoi;
Her toes curl on the sun-dried planks with senses
Charmed by the nostalgic smell of tar and sea . . .
What do a professor's visions mean to me?
But I must know these gods with moods of men,
Of whom he speaks as though they were old friends,
Their passions matched by power to satisfy
Their wildest appetite. A country's gods
Make understandable men's thoughts and deeds:
Space-man or Saint Augustine makes no odds,
We all of us build cities for our gods.

Does this imply that we invented them?
Why should I fall for such a stratagem?
It is most vexing now in this first dawn
To question what I've known since I was born:
A fundamental one, indeed, the question -
Did gods or men come first? With the suggestion
That if we see gods only through men's eyes,
Which seems agreed, then it's a pack of lies
To make up stories that the gods came first;
As wise to say that water makes you thirst.
Yet, having got the gods, the usual way
For men in search of comfort is to pray
To what they've long or recently invented,
A practise that in this case seems demented.
A scientist awaiting signs propitious
From a computer is as superstitious
As any man who tenders an oblation
Propitiating gods of his creation.
But men still use the phrase 'a god's-eye view'

For superhuman vision of the true,
And, lacking power themselves to compass it,
A power greater than their own admit.

That other don, there, could he answer this?
Dare I disturb the unencumbered bliss
Of Simpkin, torso naked in a chair,
Unintellectual in the sun-kissed air?
Sweet-sour as pickled cucumbers in brine,
His greenish eyes look sharply into mine.
   'Have you considered that six hours will bring
   You to the cliff of the Castalian Spring?
   No, sir, I'll not push out my coracle
   On seas ruled by the Delphic Oracle.'

The undulating hours pass: now clothed,
Professor Simpkin dissipates time with his wit,
While glass-and-bottle clink accompanies the notes
Made by the studious as other drowse:
Then, when at length the ship rides in Itea bay,
A murmuring quiet falls: the land-led people
Move as the blind might with slow-dawning sight,
Wondering at what till now their ears have named.
High in the steep valley, where Parnassos' peaks
And the Pheidriades reflect hot, silver light,
I let them go and enter a museum room.

There, in that cool white empty place, alone
In the deep stillness of suspended tumult,
Stands the bronze young charioteer, victorious;
His head still windswept by the gale of death,
He asks with dazed eyes how it is he lives;
Right hand extended, broken ribbons clasped,
He seems to tender, rather than accept, the prize.
Thus, after more than two millenniums,

He questions. Yet I expect an answer.
Beyond through an arch a frieze of gods,
Debating who should win the Trojan war,
Brings to three goddesses a private joke;
Their heads incline with laughing backward looks that follow
me.

The noon sleep passes and the olive tree
Stirs its slender leaves, trunk and leaves silver
As the air-shimmer that makes a river
Of the road that runs to Delphi;
Beyond, where it bends and vanishes,
Oedipus unknowing slew his father
Three thousand years ago, if one recalls
That Theseus, protecting Oedipus when blind,
Already had destroyed the Minotaur in Crete . . .
I? Recall? Too much, too soon, bemuses me.
I will follow that cool chuckle from the trees
That calls me off into the violet quiet
Of undemanding groves, with leaves lacing
A lawn beside a real substantive spring.

It sings! It sings! And the leaves whispering
Make music with the limpid, crystal stream
That dances down the Castalian cliff;
But no bird song, no flutter from the trees.
My eyes struggle with their heavy lids . . .
Did the Spring babble always then as now
From infinitely far, yet lucidly?
A voice persistently intrudes my quiet:
    'You have not ventured in this place before?'
I have no answer, tongue-tied by the spell
Of running water turned to words;
But, as she overbends the stream,
Conjure Odysseus' words to Nausicaa,
Perfection like to Leto's fresh, young palm.

The girl turned, wet sparks flying from her hands;
White-armed, dark-haired, her speculative eyes
Possessed Callisto's subtle tireless look,
Callisto, guide for voyagers ashore,
Construing with her sensuous scholarship
The lectures of the disputatious dons.
Moving, she spoke again.
                              'Then follow me
   'Before the crowd comes to the Sanctuary.
   You do not know Apollo's pedigree?'
   I said, 'I know some slight mythology.
   'May I admire the peplos that you wear?'
   She answered, as my voice were soundless,
                                                'Here

   'Before Apollo was another,
   Gaia, the Earth-Mother
   Who employed the Python
   As her shrine's guardian.'
   'The serpent Ophion-Boreas?'
   'A variant. Apollo slew him as
   Retaliation for great Hera's
   Treatment of his mother, Leto
   Hera, Zeus' wife, was never slow
   In jealously and punishment
   Of Zeus' mistresses; Zeus had lent
   To Leto the same quail's semblance
   As he used to couple with her in a sacred dance,
   So Hera ordered Python on a chase
   To see she found no nesting-place.
   You'll hear at Delos how she found one there,
   Was able after nine days to bear
   Apollo who pursued and slew the Python at Parnassos:
   Here by the Shining Rocks . . .'

A summer silence filled the wood.

'How did he come so far?' I asked.
'As a dolphin from the Cyclades,
Arching and leaping to a ship
Whose sailors, dumbly worshipping,
Turned back from Crete to bring him,
The Delphinian Apollo.'
'I've heard that tale, though some say
He came cross-country from the north,
Homer tells both, Euripides another.'
'You would prefer to see these tales
As parables of history,
Invaders bringing their own gods
Who then perform the acts of men?'
'But where's the borderline?'

The air was sun-blazed at the wood's end.
    'There is the omphalos, the earth's navel,'
Said the girl, outfacing the light
That struck sand-pink eroded pillars
Rising above the olive sea
That lapped a plateau by the Sacred Way.
The crowd was there before us
Panting stubbornly in silence,
With Callisto the Greek guide beckoning
While her lips framed soundless words.
I smiled at those I knew, passing
The Epigoni and the Argive kings,
But they looked past me; near the temple
Was a round, pressed floor, the girl spoke
And they turned their heads towards Callisto;
Still, I thought how much alike the two seemed.
We walked in a white-gold nimbus
Exhaled by the sun-white rocks.

    'Here is the halōs where each year

Apollo slays the serpent in a mime,
Here, he fought Dionysos for the shrine
That neither won. The virtue
Of their oracles remains the same;
So by Apollo's golden statue is inscribed
"Here lies dead Dionysos, son of Semele".'

'Do the gods then die?'

'Only by dying can new life arise,
No spring without an autumn death
As there can be no harvest without seed.
For half a year Apollo yields the shrine,
Dionysos returns to us each spring:
Apollo is a god of intellect,
"Know thyself!" and "Nothing in excess!"
Are cut into the wall there by the Way,
Along with musical notations for a dance
To suit the style of Dionysos . . .
'He of the green fruit,' she sang, 'god of the vines
And all the senses, corn and pines,
Fathering on Aphrodite Priapus,
The phallic, fecund god from Lampsacus;
Apollo with the dark god divides
Our nature, with curb chain rides
The conflict of the mind and senses;
Dionysos recompenses
From his passionate divinity
Mankind's godlike creativity . . .'

There was a Maenad light in her eye,
Her voice Ionian as the bees of Priapus
Who love the god in the full glare
Too bright for me fearful of such ecstasy.
    'You were saying,' I said, 'that we are near the shrine

Where stands the tripod for the Pythoness,
The place of vapours and the oracle.
Shall we go there now before the crowds?'
She sighed then like a summer breeze:
    'The golden tripod is gone
    From its column of three serpents twined,
    And the column taken by Constantine
    To his Byzantine Hippodrome.'
She pointed to the temple's pillared ramp:
    'There will be time for that experience
    When night blends future, past and present tense.'

She moved cool and easy as I scrambled
Puffed though not sweating in the siccate air,
With the figs dropping by the bouldered way
And a wild passion-flower among the stones;
We paused by the theatre's tiered arc,
Where, sun-entranced, some faithful followers
Inhaled the Ion of Euripides;
Professor Tarragon's intoning voice
Pursued through two millenniums and a half
To reach the passionate stern Attic pitch,
Its trancy Celtic rise and fall
In lovely lingering sound pursued us,
Till at length we stood in silence
By the stone seats of the stadium,
Tier upon tier above cascading green,
Olive- and fig-green falling steeply,
Deeply down the limestone
To the Pleistos lost in powdery haze,
And peaks like islands floating, a new land,
Arcadia, beyond the Corinth Gulf.

Silence of afternoon's late shimmering,
With cool shadow on hot rocks suspending,

The first whispering of light airs casting
Thoughts inscrutable as spirits passing,
Silence of the high-borne eagle drifting
And the hollow in the air soft-closing
On the sudden bleat of kid despairing,
Silent Parnassian spurs now shielding
North, east and west, so that the westering
Sun lit peaks alone, with all else darkening.

The hard-stamped sandy floor,
A table cut into the mountainside,
Ran east to west two hundred yards,
An empty hanging garden for the Games,
With blocks for the hard feet thrusting
When the hand dropped or the trumpet blew
And away went the oiled nude bodies,
Running for the glory of Apollo;
But, for the laurel chaplet, nomes were sung
To flute and lyre as Hermes used to make
From reeds and shell of tortoise for Apollo:
So to Apollo now the hymns were sung.

'Terpander made such music,'
Said the girl, 'and Pindar with his lyrics,
'Later nomes were more like dithyrambs
And so more fitting for Dionysos.'
'Were ever women here?' 'Not married ones.
Apollo's priestesses were at the Games,
It was their sacred duty to be here:
Some scholars say the Games were secular,
But you will take no heed of that.'

Down, with the twilight sliding on the slopes,
Sharp stones slipping, the theatre empty,
Reclining on its tiers to stare grey-mouthed

Above contorted olives, and ripe figs
Purpled-plopping on the hot, crumbled earth.
The temple area was last-light luminous;
Corroded fluted columns of drum stones
Set on each other like firm, pillared buns
Pink-nibbled by millenniums of mice
Held the reflection of the setting sky.
Passing the length until the eastern end,
The girl went up on to the temple floor,
Facing the omphalos, the navel of the world.
And there she sat, I thought upon a tripod,
Posture upright, seated, hands upon her knees,
With her lips moving as though to speak,
Or chewing the laurel leaves, I thought.
A mist was rising, from the mist her voice
Came as I had first heard it, quiet close
Yet distant, now suffusing the cool air,
The vespertine still universe that watched
The passing of one more unnumbered sun.

'A thousand years men came to me,
Knowing my oracle to be
The truth: no man would venture
Any plan, nor make indenture
Without my knowledge or advice:
My utterances repeated thrice
The priest attendant to hexameters reduced;
The priestessess were virgin, till one was seduced,
Since when no woman under fifty is installed,
Though still by title of Apollo's bride she's called.'

'But, you . . . '

'You are a stranger here and to our gods,
Their bloody rage and passions when Zeus nods;

Apollo is a priest of his own rite,
Son, husband, numinous hermaphrodite;
The Great Mother you will find in Delos,
The greatest of her shrines in Ephesos,
Only in Delphi is Apollo free
Of the incestuous matriarchy.
But many gods and goddesses you'll meet,
Zeus, Hera his sister-wife, much tried, discreet
Protectress of the home; their son Haephestos
Married Aphrodite, lovely and promiscuous,
Who with his brother slept, Ares, the god of war,
A handsome, drunken brute, a most vile avatar:
And then Poseidon, powerful and lecherous . . .
Be warned that almost all of them are treacherous;
In short, their qualities you'll find
Within the breasts of most mankind;
Without the gods there'd be no history to write,
No history, no lore of gods to light
Man's evolution. Have you a request?
The days before you will provide a test.'
The light was passing and the mist more dense,
A stupefying smoke that scrambled sense.
　'But yes!' I cried, 'Now that I'm setting forth,
How to ensure I get my money's worth?'

Oracular answer hexameter paronomastic,
　'A man gets from life what he gives, his chance
　　　　　　　　　　　　　　is therefore elastic.'

　　　　　　　　　　　　　　　　　'Fantastic,
　'How time stretches like elastic.
Since when have you been dozing by the Spring?'
'Dozing?' I asked. 'You saw us following
'Callisto, the Greek guide who led the crowd.'
'Did you see me? And did she speak out loud?'

'There was a passion-flower beside the Way -
You saw it, too?' 'Yes, near the agora.'
'Then I was surely there! That's proof enough.'
My love said, 'Take my hand, the path is rough
'And dark among these planes; I've read that near
By the Meander at Magnesia
There is a tree not far from Ephesos
Where lives a likeness of Dionysos.'

II

Olympia - The Curse of Atreus - Nestor receives Telemachus at
Pylos.

All night the ship sailed on a tranquil sea
And came to Katokolo at that hour
When swimming was a larkspur sport for gods,
The air a little smelling of the dark,
Serene yet salty, drawn by the first sun
From grey, smooth wavelets that caressed my arms
And left translucent jewels on my skin:
When later, with a hot wind off the shore,
We climbed where greenness had survived from spring,
There spread quite suddenly a valley's lawn
Deep in the hills' hollow, with a bright stream
In the still pale morning, stilly waiting
For our coming. A sun-filtering haze,
Filling a pine grove with blue, shimmering light,
Contained the silence of suspended sound.

So this is Olympia, where time stays
Motionless as if it were to-day the sanctuary
Was found beneath a thousand years of silt.
Fondly, the Alpheus and Cladeus
Covered each year with floods tumultuous
The altis spoiled by Theodosius:
Byzantines, then Franks, stayed here awhile,
But floods returned and lava-like
Mud seeped, grew deeper, ever deeper . . .
The Hermes of Praxiteles leaned further,
Gently swooned with soft squelch in the turgid ooze,

Sinking, sinking while nearby Apollo,
Standing between the Lapiths and the Centaurs,
Felt the slow topple of his pediment
And so submersed, as also slipped
The Nike of Paionios from her pedestal;
Only the great archaic head of Hera,
Long since buried by its weight, lay immobile:
Last to slide slyly in seducing slough,
Went Zeus gaily grasping Ganymede . . .

Then a long, closed silence,
Opened only by the sighing fall
Of temples, sucking of spring waters
And dry tick of summer-baking mud;
In the fall of the year and winter, quiet absolute.
Each year, each century the silt grows
Till the very rivers are contained by it;
Then birds' droppings and the blown seed
Bring flowers, grass binds and tree-roots probe,
Though never so deep
As to wake from sleep
The gods.

Strangely, the greatest of them all escaped
And so was lost to all posterity,
Chryselephantine Zeus, world wonder,
Contrived by Phidias of gold and ivory,
And seated on a throne of bronze and ebony,
So huge that had he risen to his feet
His head had gone clear through the temple-roof,
(Strabo derided this uncalled-for spoof)
Was taken by the Christian Theodosius
And later in Byzantium was burned;
A better fate than that considered
By the oafish emperor Caligula,

Who thought of taking it to Rome
And there to change the god's head for his own.
So passed the Zeus of Phidias
Nine centuries after it was wrought,
While at Olympia, safe in mud,
The others waited fourteen hundred years
Before returning to this vale of tears.

    'Poor Winkelmann,' professor Simpkin said,
    'He longed to burrow here; his *Kunst des Altertums*
    Is still among the best *Geschichte*. But, alas!
    He died stabbed by a silly scamp, Arcangeli,
    Symbolic name for such a devil's pawn,
    Who grabbed some coins given him in honour
    By Maria Theresa in Vienna.
    So, yet another hundred years went by
    Before more scholars of his race
    Revealed the prospects of this place;
    Germanic thoroughness, if lacking wit,
    Can do some fruitful things, one must admit:
    The French had meanwhile ferreted a few
    Triglyphs for the Louvre, the bishop of Corfu,
    A cardinal of France,
    Had earlier by chance
    First traced Olympia below the hill of Cronos . . .'

The Cronion, sacred hill of Cronos,
Titan cannibal father of Zeus!
Heights close in this valley of Alpheus;
Distant Cyllene and Erymanthus
Snow-blue embrace its bowered fertility,
Making a sacred precinct of greenness.
The heart of it in this hill, conical,
Rising out of the dark of creation,
Spies on its dread and passionate children,
The gods and their quarrelsome spawn, mankind.

Here lies man's tragic, warring destiny
To be part god while living humanly:
For after the blind dance of Eurynome
When high swept the sky and deep sank the sea,
Before there was light to brand his ravishing,
Heaven, Uranus, coupled with the Earth
And begot the Titans. Cronos, last-born,
Taught by his mother to hate Uranus,
Gelded his father when he was sleeping
And flung his genitals into the sea;
Born of the fountained foam as they fell,
Rode Aphrodite on a scallop-shell.

Cronos then ruled over the Universe,
Terrified of his parents' prognosis
That one of his sons would usurp his throne:
So, as each child was born he swallowed it,
Hestia, Demeter, Hera, Hades,
Poseidon, till finally Zeus was born.
Zeus' mother, Rhea, resolved to save him,
Had him suckled by the goat Amalthea,
Swaddling a stone for Cronos to gulp.
Zeus, who had grown in strength precociously,
Brought unknown to his father metheglin
Laced with mustard which Cronos vomited,
Throwing up the stone and the children too.
Even as Cronos roared to the Titans
To come to help him preserve his throne,
The godling children grew to full stature
And hurled themselves on the hulking crew.

'A frightful conflict then began,
Like something recently devised by man,
In which there was a vast explosion;
Flames tore the dark and churned the ocean,

Rocks from the mountain tops were wrenched
As the hands of the Titans tore and clenched;
Then Zeus released the Cyclopes
To crush the Titans to their knees,
The giants with the Hundred Hands rushed out,
And, suddenly, came the Goat-god's shout
That swept the Titans with Panic rout:
With Cronos stunned by a thunder-bolt,
The gods concluded their grand revolt.
So Zeus became the Lord of Heaven,
Warding man's destiny, the leaven
Of nature and supreme law-giver,
Power-bound by Fate's mysterious river.'

Professor Simpkin gave a smiling cough.
   'Well, there's the story, not a pretty one,
But, as with roots that deeply probe,
It has strange shoots that may be gay
Or childish or sophisticate,
Or give a clue to Freud
Who put a girdle round the earth
Of tramlines for his sex-bound car.
There's food enough for thought, at least
For those born in the British Isles:
It's said that Cronos, now,
Is where Zeus banished him
Upon an island off the western coast . . .'

Then he was gone, while the crowd buzzed
Hummingly as bees in the warm, blue shade
Drone homing to a dream of dew;
Some wandered to the Leonidaeum,
Some to the stadium of Hercules,
Six hundred feet of Hercules' own pacing
Said by Pythagoras to be too long.

Seated on a stone, I ponder Tarragon,
Who, during Simpkin's discourse, seemed remote,
Still as the air about him
By the altar of Zeus' grandson, Pelops.
An elusive and fastidious don,
Yet gaudy sometimes as a peacock
In his eye-tailed words:
What does the sun hatch now
Behind the veiled lightning of his eyes?

Now he moves nearer to the shade,
Leaning his wild, fair head against an ilex,
Saying with a loose gesture,
                              'Wait!
  'You have heard only the story of the gods:
  Here at Olympia the world of men
  Is first displayed as an eccyclema,
  The new device invented by the Greeks
  Revealing what goes on behind the scenes,
  The causes and results of what is obvious.
  Watch, but do not think yourselves spectators;
  Though names you hear will be familiar,
  The tragedy is yours as much as theirs
  And purged alone through pity and through fear.'
So smiling stealthily, he looked away.
  'Relax then in the shade: your time will come.
  Your drama starts with Tantalus, Zeus' son,
  A stepping-stone between the gods and men,
  Who served his own son, Pelops, to the gods
  For dinner, hoping to please them:
  Zeus punished him with everlasting thirst.
  This nightmare figure, bobbing on the edge of myth,
  Grew from some early ritual of kings;
  For that Pelops, marvellously saved,
  Was the invading king of Lydia,
  Who sailing westward to Arcadia

Won its king's daughter Hippodamia,
In a chariot race by bribing Myrtilus,
The driver for her father Oenomaus,
With promise of priority to bed
Hippodamia on their bridal night:
He broke his vow and murdered Myrtilus,
Who as he drowned cursed Pelops and his house.

So Pelops ruled all south of Corinth,
Peloponnese it has been called since then,
(They say his were the first Olympic Games)
And, when he died at Mycenae,
Left two sons, Atreus and Thyestes;
The first succeeded, but his wife Aerope
Made him a cuckold with his brother's help:
Atreus first banished Thyestes,
Then, promising him pardon,
Lured him to a banquet of his own sons
Slain and boiled. Thyestes, sickened,
Laid a curse upon his brother's seed.

The cycle of sin, sin begetting sin,
Is set, the problem of evil posed:
Thyestes, told by the Delphic Oracle
That a son begotten on his daughter
Will assure revenge, seduces her
In darkness by her temple-pool.
Atreus pursuing meets and marries her,
And when her child, Aegisthus, is born,
He thinks the boy is his and makes him heir,
Not Agamemnon nor Menelaus,
Sons by his slain, adulterous wife.
Soon, when he has Thyestes in his power,
He sends the boy to kill him,
But Thyestes knows Aegisthus for his son
And sends him back to murder Atreus:

23

Prophecy's fulfilled, and evil keeps its course.
Thyestes reigns somewhile until his nephew
Agamemnon drives him out with Aegisthus:
Agamemnon, now king of kings,
Has married Clytemnestra, Leda's daughter;
Menelaus, his brother, made no happier choice
In marrying her sister Helen,
Who submitted willingly enough
To Paris in his mis-called rape.

So, there begins the Trojan War:
Agamemnon, with the Argive fleets
Becalmed at Aulis at the start,
Makes sacrifice of Iphigenia,
His child and Clytemnestra's; the wind
Changes and the war proceeds. Meanwhile, at home
His queen takes Aegisthus his cousin to her bed;
Their passion, composite of love
And common hatred for the king,
Is pitiless. So, when Troy falls
And Agamemnon comes victorious,
Bringing Cassandra with him,
He is taken in a net, stabbed by his wife,
Cassandra murdered with her twins.
The children of the murdered king,
Orestes exiled and Electra brooding,
Wait their moment to avenge their father:
When it comes, Orestes kills Aegisthus,
And, in the courtyard, his own mother
On the stones where she had killed Cassandra.'

Professor Tarragon stopped suddenly:
His heat-borne words rose slowly in the trees,
Then swayed like hanged men while the people stared.

'Here is the frightful sublety of sin.
You gasp with horror at this massacre?
Of course: but when the killer, Clytemnestra,
Gives her reasons for it, you accept them.
Agamemnon killed their daughter,
And returning brings his mistress;
Divine will cries retribution,
No matter an adulteress
Has now become a murderess,
She, Clytemnestra, has done justice,
Brought home the sinner's sin to him.
Must we despair then of humanity,
When men and women in the acts of others
Find spurious vindication of their own?
Can there be for us some further act
To bring this tragic sequence to an end?
Can only gods conclude what man has set in train,
Or will man sometimes learn from suffering and pain?
Orestes fled the Black Erinnyes, serpent-haired,
Bat-winged Furies punishing kin-murder,
Holding his bloody hands to his tormented head
He cowered condemned, then wandered mad
With hands unwashed from killing
Till Athene summoned him to trial,
Aeschylus says Orestes was absolved
At Athens by the Areopagus,
At which Athene gave her casting vote.
Call it then destiny or fate,
Or man at last appalled by hate:
See that the lesson is not learned too late . . .'

His ending sank so deep, it caught my breath
To know the world might hate itself to death.
Where is Tarragon now? I turn and stare.
My love directs her pencil where

He stands with closed eyes in the shade,
Hearing the noisy spirits fade
And holding to his private vision.
She speaks to me with mild precision:
    'Your head is hot, the sun is climbing high.'

So, by the hearth of Hestia we lay,
Listening to a pine tree's prickly sigh
And flutter of noon-silent birds at play.
Had they, had I . . . what was it I had seen?
How could there be this deep tranquillity
While the sweet ether kept such torment green
To challenge hope in man's futurity?
Was it the Truce of God persisting here,
When, for the Games, men could address
To Zeus their minds and bodies without fear
And keep a balance, nothing in excess?
For each fourth year all fighting had to cease,
When in that month the god demanded peace.

(It seems that girl at Delphi's stadium
Was right in bidding me ignore the dictum
That Games were secular, with no te deum.)

Here in the days before Olympian Zeus,
In Pelops' time, perhaps, or Oenamaus',
When, to a mother-goddess of fertility,
The Games became a symbol of virility,
This place was sacred, dedicated,
Man with his body gods placated.
Then, as he grew, his highest aim in living
Was to have mind and body close agreeing,
And so become a balanced, seamless being.

(Quattrocento Mantuan virtu
Perceived the wit of it,

The public schools of England, too,
Tried soon to copy it:
But still the Ageless Ones are jealous of old age,
Grown wisdom challenging their own induces rage;
Maybe that's why those whom the gods love do die young,
And why so many men, like me, remain unsung.)

Such and such dizzy, shimmering thoughts
Simmered in the cool oven of the shade,
Till presently we bumped sedately
Through the Balkan countryside,
Like yet unlike the hills of Italy
Where man's persistent hand is evident
In sheltering tapered trees and fruitful groves,
The very cliffs of savage Appenine
Transformed by nightingales to make a garden.
But here, when gods retreated to Olympus,
Leaving the world to anarchy and fear,
Nature and time connived to make a wild:
The vales, grown thick to hide the fugitives
From man's Greek effort to be civilised,
Conceal the shrines whose groves, reduced to scrub,
Flung on the wind their seeds to fertilize
Another culture, once more on the run.
Eagles, not nightingales, here make their nests,
Circling the steely, haunted crests.

Late afternoon we came to Nestor's home,
Palace of Pylos of which Homer tells,
There's now a little seaport of that name,
The palace is at Englianos -
There's always been confusion on this score.
Nestor, who in old age became a bore,
A royal, Polonius prototype,
Was wise and in his youth athletic;

C

Born to the Nelean house of Messene kings,
He ruled three generations' span:
So, when these ruins were disclosed
Before the last World War . . . (Which one?
Not long ago: I was a man.)
The archaeologists declared that
This, for all its crumbled glory,
Must be his; no man but Nestor
Had such wealth and style.

There was an evening perfume as we climbed the hill,
Musky and damp, yet dusty,
Ticklish as dried mint in our throats.
Was there a smell of burning in the air?
It seemed so, though the sea below
Sent up its evening west wind whispering
Among the low walls, through the propylon
To the Throne room by the inner court,
Playing with visions of the mind's eye
On painted, fluted columns,
Frescoed griffins backed by lions,
And up the stairs to balconies
From which the jars of olive oil had dropped
To feed the burning, baking the tablets.

The tablets are heaped in the archives room,
Their message in the clay preserved by fire,
Spelling the dry facts piece by piece
To tell the urgency of danger,
Yet no word of what that danger is:
Appointments are noted here of watchers
To the Hither and the Further Provinces,
The rowers that will guard the coastline gaps,
The disposition of the women and the children
Drawn back for safety in the towns,

Storing of corn and rations for emergency,
Masons to strengthen the defences,
Bronze-workers to convert the temple bronze
To spears and arrows. Here's a story
Of intense haste, and detail measured
To prepare a desperate stand.
They were the last words of the Greek Bronze Age.
The sudden enemy swept over it
And put Nestor's great palace to the flames:
No one has lived there for three thousand years.

From what chaotic Asiatic hole
The Dorian invaders came is still discussed:
Five centuries of twilight followed them,
Only in unconquered Athens lived
A fading recollection of Mycenaean things,
And bards who passed from mouth to mouth
Through centuries the stories Homer found:
What else was left of culture fled abroad
To found Ionian cities
In that lovely Asia whence disaster came.

Yet, but a hundred years before,
This palace and its king were at their peak:
Old Nestor had not long returned from Troy
Whither he'd taken ninety long black ships;
There, wise Nestor, Gerenian charioteer,
Tamer of horses and unrivalled counsellor,
Of all men most admired by Agamemnon,
Was hand-in-glove with sly Odysseus,
Who, younger, had but little less of craft
And with him had contrived the victory.

So when Telemachus, Odysseus' son,
Came with the north wind in his sails
From Ithaca to seek his father,

Missing many years since Troy,
Old Nestor welcomed him and all his crew,
Made sacrifice and feasted him
With a heifer whose young horns
The palace goldsmith had adorned to please Athene.

There in the still blue eve
I smelled the hungry, spiralled smoke
As the king threw red wine on the flames,
And the young men with their five-pronged forks
Crouched with the spitted meat before the fire;
It was in my nostrils as I turned
To see Odysseus' son,
Fresh from the bath
Where Nestor's youngest daughter, Polycaste,
Had rubbed his smooth young skin with oil,
And dressed him in so fine a cloak and tunic
He appeared as lovely as a god.

He feasted, listened: Nestor had no news,
But sent him on straightway
With long-maned horses and a chariot
With his own son, Peisistratus,
To take him to the red-haired Menelaus,
Who, with Helen long returned from Troy,
Received him royally until Athene
Hastened his return to Ithaca . . .

The pattern-painted terracotta bath is there,
And in a corner two jars open to the air,
The oil is dried, no water fills the well,
But Polycaste the beautiful will dwell
Young as Telemachus, immortally,
With Nestor's kindness, gracefully
Enshrined in Homer's Odyssey, Book Three.

III

Night voyage to Piraeus - Professor Tarragon on Niobe,
nightingales and swallows.

There was no moon, and the unruffled sea
Was iridescent where the ship's light fell
On water slipping from a dolphin's tail
Parting the sea like opening a book
And closing it without a page disturbed.
So silently and smooth we slipped away
From the serenity of Pylos' bay:
(More frequently now Navarino called,
After a battle when the Turks were stalled)
Sphacteria lies close across its mouth,
Leaving a passage where the water's deep:
Nearing this island forested by night
I felt his watching, even in the dark,
Waiting for some sound beyond the ear's reach.
Most men are noted for the sounds they make,
The few, like this professor Tarragon,
For silence emanating waves of sense
That know a super-sensual world.

    'I hoped that I might hear the nightingale,'
He murmured. 'But the year is late?' I asked.
'Not for the brown one, Aëdon,' he sighed,
And then was silent. 'Here especially,'
He said presently, 'because of Niobe.'

His thought was travelling too fast for me:
It seemed indeed he spoke more to the night,

Unravelling some puzzle in his mind,
Indifferent, nor displeased that I was there.
  'How fearful are the crimes of jealousy!
Assassin and antipodes of love,
  Yet sometimes sprung from it, like bastard hate.'
Remembering a vision in the sun,
I ventured,
    'Tantalus? The curse again?'
  'One does seem fated to return to it,'
Said Tarragon. 'Aëdon's father,
  'Pandareus, had conspired with Tantalus,
Therefore the gods destroyed him:
Aëdon married Zethus whose twin
Amphion wed Pelops' sister, Niobe;
The brothers were twin kings of Thebes.
Niobe had fourteen children,
Unhappy Aëdon had one;
Made mad by jealousy,
She tried to kill Niobe's eldest son,
But in the envious dark of night
She slew Itylus, her only child.
In pity Zeus transformed her to the nightingale
Who sings eternally her silvery lament.'

'Why here, and why because of Niobe?'

'Because . . . Poor, lovely queen of Thebes,
Here seven sons and seven daughters
Made her so proud she dared compare herself
With Leto who had only two.
The goddess at this blasphemy
Despatched Apollo and his sister,
Artemis, with swift-avenging bows
To slay all but one boy and girl who'd prayed to her.
So was Niobe punished for her pride,

And wept and wept and nothing comforted:
Observing this was more than flesh could bear,
Zeus turned her to a stone on Sipylus.
The daughter who'd escaped wed Neleus
The Messene king who reigned at Pylos,
Their one surviving son was Nestor:
So Aëdon, the brown nightingale,
Comes here to sing lament for all the children
Slain by jealousy and pride and war,
Here, near the last survivor of her clan.'

The ship turned south, the dolphin-water hissed,
The island filled with silent song lay dark
Upon the still, steel pool embraced and hidden
By the mainland's hills and mountains, where
From a sheltered crest old Nestor's palace watched.

  'You'd think Zeus might have intervened,'
  Said Tarragon. 'Leto was his love,
  'Her children his. Instead, he pitied.
  What use is pity when it comes too late?'
  'You take it very seriously.'
  'The gods are mirrors to ourselves;
  Sometimes they let things take their course,
  Preferring not to be involved.'
  'As in the Philomel and Procne myth?'
  'Humans and birds share many qualities,
  Spite and lust markedly,' said Tarragon,
  'Though in that tale the nightingale
  And swallow both are innocents betrayed.'

  I said, 'At Ludlow once in June
  'I saw a mask, the light of a full moon
  Blent with the lamps to ease the dusk darkling;
  The wild flexuous swallows circling
  Screamed at the "Wood-entranced chaste-footing maid"

Their warning of the charms by Comus laid,
Such as " 'Tis only day-light that makes Sin";
So, when the contest came, she stayed virgin,
Seduced *him* with a song of nightingale
Who sang, "in violet imbroider'd vale",
"Thou canst not touch the freedom of my minde".'

               'The optimists who lead mankind,'
Said the professor, 'are the English;
'Innocence from good they can't distinguish.
There is a charm,' he sighed, 'in innocence,
Especially considered in past tense:
But here the light's too sharp and too revealing,
Remember that in case you think of stealing
Shards, poultry or a pretty maidenhead;
The gods are quick to judgement - and you're dead!'
His silent laughter reached me, then his head
Was suddenly alert. 'What's that?' he said.
  'A squeaking, sun-dried warp, no siren dread!'
  'Then till to-morrow, when the Parthenon
Is wed to a blue-mantled dawn upon
Athene's helm that shines to Sunion!'

IV

Athens Acropolis - The Eleusinian Mysteries - Tarragon on Phryne —
Terrible as an army with banners.

The mantle of the honied Parthenon
Is misty hyaline, a burning glass
That leaves the mind no flocculent, damp thoughts;
The sun, that in the dawn an hour since
Had warmed my body streaming from the sea,
Now sears the night-storm saturated stones
Of the Acropolis, vaporizing,
Levitating the tremendous temples,
So weighty, yet so lightly tremulous
To float skyward, sublimate in space.

Propylaea's pentelic pillars,
White, warmed by weather, soar beside me,
Making a great gateway for the sun
To burnish the feet-polished rocks
That climb the Panathenaic Way
To the Erectheum, where once Athene waited
Each third year of the Olympiad
When rocks were July burnished:
Prancing horses clopped and sandals slapped
In the cacophonous procession,
Splendid with the ship-borne woven peplos
For the goddess, hailing on its way
Her huge, bronze statue, Promachos,
Whose golden spear-point gleamed
Through the Athenian sky to summon
Sailors off the point of Sunion.

Then, at the Erectheum, Ionic,
Feminine, they found their very roots:
Here was the rock split by Poseidon
To maintain his claim to Attica,
Here, by the western wall, the olive tree
Athene planted to support her view
That wisdom has a higher claim than force;
She won the gods' approval by one vote,
Although Poseidon keeps an altar there,
Smith-god Hephaestos and Erectheos,
Too; cthonic is the tomb of Cecrops,
Earth-born, half-serpent ancestor of kings.

'Erectheus or Ericthonius,'
Professor Simpkin's mood seems captious:
'The ancients muddled them, so why should we
Presumptuously dissect their pedigree,
Whichever name you choose there were two men,
Each one a part of history or myth;
Somewhere between them came king Pandion,
Father of Procne and Philomela
Whose brother Aegeus was tricked, they say,
Into begetting Theseus. Pelop's son,
The marriage of whose daughter Aethra
Had fallen through, made Aegeus drunk
And led him to her bed. Later that night
She woke and went to find another love,
Poseidon; so one really is not sure
Who fathered Theseus - or any of us
Come to that. Man or god? A question rare.'
He laughs, and snaps his fingers at the air.

I move away towards the Parthenon:
The morning's gossamer that filters gold
From the young sun swims through the high doorway,
Swooning and swelling among the pillars

In a slow dance towards the western end.
For a breath I know the cella empty,
Then, behind the altar of the goddess,
The unwreathing spiral of the mist
Reveals the tall Athene Parthenos,
Gold, ivory and ebony soaring
To the roof, and around the walls the frieze
Of the riders beautifully seated,
Reining their prancers with chlamys blowing
And sea-tossed manes of four-horse chariots;
Here sober attitudes of older men
And of suppliant girls with plattered gifts;
Here fat young heifers led to sacrifice,
Some patient, others fearful scenting blood
Pull back, tails up, rearing with flared nostrils.
Thus the Panathenaic Procession
Canters, strides and paces with the peplos
To drape the virgin sprung from Zeus' head,
Watched by a group of lounging, jealous gods.

Strange how the wispy mists distort the shapes!
They are a part of the sky, and an apse
Swells out behind Athene who has changed
To an anno domini sixth century
Virgin Mother of God, Theotokos;
A light breeze stirs ecclesiastic dust
To wrap her in an airy spiral sheath,
Leaving the temple empty, while transformed
To minaret she soars above the roof,
Apostrophising yet another change.
But still the same frieze gazes down,
A little lacking through adversity,
Unweathered, though . . . My palms pressed to my ears
I step back quickly on the cringing toe
Of one of the professor's followers;
Her gasp and Simpkin's sharp-eyed voice unite

In condemnation of such violence.

'The frightful blast in 1687
Threw down columns, blew the roof to heaven;
The Turks had made the Parthenon a store
For powder, and by accident of war
A shell from the Venetians landed Plop!
And for a century or more a stop
Was put to building up the ruined shrine,
Save that a mosque stood on the cella's line.
But then Lord Elgin, breathe his name with pride,
Although some people take the other side,
Obtained a firman from the Turks to save
The fallen frieze and sculpture from the wave
Of squalor, dust and local unconcern;
The question now is if we should return
What but for Elgin would have long been lost
Instead of cherished at enormous cost.
The argument will go ad nauseam,
The while the marbles stay in the B.M..
The archaeologists, their native pride
Apart, are apt when questioned to confide
Their view the frieze is safer where it is,
An attitude that all are free to quiz.'

Soft-soled susurrating shoes sigh smoothly,
Weaving through the weathered columns:
Where was my love gone now?
Should I return to the Erectheum,
Empty, sun-dried white, with purple shadows
On the shoulders of the Caryatids?
Like bees approaching home, more people crawl
Through the Propylaea, moving singly
Or in hundred groups across the polished rock
Towards the Parthenon, yet with no sound
Except a murmuring from the hive of tongues

As there has ever been in this high place,
The eye of Attica and of the world,
Made for great concourse and absorbing it.

A dark head sculptured on a pale blue sky
Between two icy pillars takes my eye:
So, to a fallen capital nearby,
I go to catch the centuries that fly
Down to the distant hollow in hilled
Aegaleos, where the torchlight filled
The late September night and thrilled
The catachumens for Eleusis, stilled
Their breath, invoking love of Iacchos
Born aloft, the youthful Dionysos.

    The dark head turned. 'You're whispering again,'
                            she said.
   'Be still, here in the shade, and tell instead
   Of how the road down to the far plain led
   To Eleusinian Mysteries of which I've read.'

I, tell! How could I tell of Mysteries
The secrecy of which no man could speak
But in veiled language? As did Aeschylus,
Who, for his pains, was nearly torn to shreds
By those who thought him traitor to the cult
Most sacred, sung in the Homeric Hymn
In glory of Demeter and her child,
Persephone, named Kore in the rites,
Who, meadow-flower entranced, was ravished
By the god Hades of the Underworld.
The Hymn tells how Demeter came
To Eleusis, learned of her daughter's rape
By the Host of Many's chariot,
And raging wretchedly forbade the earth
To yield till Kore was returned:

39

Vainly the oxen ploughed and vain the seed
Sown, the fruit trees pruned and herb-beds tended,
Earth lay naked, barren, burned and bony
As mankind who starved till Zeus persuaded
Hades to restore Persephone,
If she'd not eaten in the lower world.
Spying her nibbling seeds of pomegranate,
The leering dark god sent her back,
Knowing she could not be away for long.

'So, named Persephone,' I said, 'sweet Kore reigns
Four pregnant winter months in Tartarus,
And comes each year with new birth in the spring,
Stays with her mother while the corn sprouts strong
And branches bend a little more each week,
Fecundate flowers fall and fruit is formed
Which swells with golden barley ripening:
As Kore is the goddess of the young corn,
So is Demeter goddess of the old
And harvests the ripe seed for Kore's womb
To nourish warmly in dark winter's sleep.

But, later, Iacchos joined the autumn rite,
The young Dionysos of Attica,
And, when September comes with shortening light,
This fair young god is borne by votaries
To Eleusis by the Sacred Way
Which goes below there to the Dipylon,
The double gate beyond Hephaestos' temple,
To the pass into the Eleusinian plain.'

She said, 'You're mixing up the story with the rite,'
'But who knows which came first?' I asked. 'A sun too
                                                white
Burns on their heads and mine, by day too bright;

And ruddy torches, swept with song at night,
Marry in man his darkness and his light.
With absolutes so fused, who knows what's right?'

I spoke like this for fear I'd gone too far:
The hymn that Homer sings was acted at Eleusis,
Performed by hierophant and dadoukos
In the deep Hall of the Initiates.
Fear of the gods inhibits memory;
Each writer wraps his knowledge in such clothes
As may disarm the watchful eye of heaven:
Only the great Clement, pagan in his youth
Then Christian father, had no scruples here,
And even he . . . If he had been initiate
Would he forget so quickly what he learned,
Or, lacking scruples, not retell the whole?
For fourteen hundred years before Christ came,
And seven centuries before the Hymn,
Demeter's Mysteries had taken place,
- The first Greek mother-goddess, earth and grain -
Yet all that's known is of a passion play
Of Kore wandering among flowers,
Abducted, and Demeter sorrowing
Divinely for her daughter, while the earth
Lies fallow, yearning for the child's rebirth,
When, with the mother's joy, all men rejoice.

Was there a birth scene of a holy child?
Was there a sacrament, the votary's
Uniting supper with divinity?
Clement has told the mystae's formula:
"I have fasted, I have drunk the barley,
From the sacred chest have taken holy things,
And, having tasted them, into the basket
Placed them for return into the chest."
But there's no savage indication found

Of men believing that they ate their god:
Only a coexisting life and death,
As Easter is and Christmas-tide rebirth.

With eyes and arms upraised they shouted "Rain!"
And gazing at the earth cried out "Conceive!"
The Mystery was then at last revealed,
The miracle of the reaped ear of corn . . .
When the sharp indrawn breath of wonder passed
There came the logos of the hierophant,
Pointing with surge of sweetly sounding words
The immortality here symbolised,
The very resurrection and the life.
No dogma and no moral homilies,
No threatened horrors of a judgement day:
Assurance came to the initiate
Through mystic concord with Demeter's child,
Mother and daughter, powers of life and death.
Was he the better for it? We must guess.
Outspoken Aristophanes said, "Yes".

'But what of Iacchos? Why was he invoked?'

My love's voice sounded cool and crystalline,
Yet undulous as thought waves always are
When thrown back, rolling from a distant shore.
I thought I had been silent since she spoke.

'Oh, Iacchos,' I said, 'child Dionysos,
Came after Athens conquest of Eleusis:
Going with shouts of "Iacche! Fecund God!"
They carried him to the night's great revel
Near the Hall before initiation.
He died as the winter Dionysos,
Awoke with vegetation in the spring;
He was the needful symbol of unreason,

A dark power to be worshipped in the dark
When nature's impulse can be loosed
With absolute abandon. He may show
Himself in cruel madness or a poet's thought,
But never, never can he be ignored;
He is imperative, the balance
To the spirit, intellect and light.
His orgy is a secret worship
Here synonymous with Mystery,
Fitting the part played in this drómena;
Obscene is sacred if it scours the soul.'

' "The lust of the goat is the bounty of God." '

The voice was Tarragon's; I turned.
He was alone, the noon sun burned
On the white column where he leaned his head.
    'It was not always mystical,' he said,
And then was silent, half-closed eyes agaze
To seek some substance in the Attic haze.
    'Poseidon, Kore's uncle, had a Feast
With rites, and, though as solemn, not the least
Like hers; it was inherent there should be
His worship at Eleusis by the sea.

    You've heard of Phryne, the great courtesan,
Whose beauty made all women also ran?
The fame established by her loveliness
Induced her at Eleusis to undress:
As Aphrodite Anadyomene,
With hair spread on her shoulders in a stream
Of gold, and standing in the sea,
Her nakedness seemed true virginity.
The watching pilgrims at this miracle
Behaved as though they'd heard an oracle.

Thus she inspired the painting by Apelles,
At least two statues by Praxiteles,
But then of profanation was accused:
Her action at Eleusis was abused
In court at Athens, where her advocate
Hyperides was from an early date
Her lover, worshipper of to kalon,
With orat'ry to kindle hearts of stone:
He'd been a pupil of Isocrates
Whose periods he capped in subtleties,
For Lysias' style he had great sympathy
And borrowed words from Middle Comedy;
In sum, a barrister of grace and wit
Whose tact unfailingly produced words fit
For any case: we may recall this man,
Of Athens has been called the Sheridan.

But now, try as he will, he makes no dent,
The judges on conviction are intent;
The sacred Mysteries have been profaned
By Phryne, who, notoriously stained,
Now stands there with a face of innocence:
Such modesty is certain to incense.
'Hoarse as he is, and almost in despair,
Hyperides has one ploy left to dare:
Both eyes on heaven, one hand upon his client,
He rips her robe, displays her body pliant;
Her blue-veined breasts, each with a supple eye
To outstare reason, make the senses fly,
Her navel like a miniscule clam shell
Set in her lily belly . . . I must tell
The judges were so moved by all this beauty,
They instantaneously performed their duty
Of any desecration to acquit her,
In showing such perfection to Demeter.'

The rock-dust smelled of fire and hot, crushed thyme.

'Fair, forever, as the moon is she; clear as the sun,
Terrible as an army with banners,' said Tarragon.

A strayed goat bleated near the shrine of Pan,
Set in the rocks to honour Pan's appearance
To Pheidippides the runner seeking help
Before the fight at Marathon.
So, in a great cloud of dust, had Iacchos come
To cheer the Grecian camp at Salamis,
Borne on the wind from Eleusis.

The dust was in my throat, and dark my sight
In the white light as of a sun-bright night:
My love sat silently discreet and neat,
Hearing the shuffle of unnumbered feet.

V

Mykonos, Lotus-eating - Simpkin and Tarragon at odds over
interpretation of Artemis on Delos - Callisto reappears:
Tarragon's obsession - Strange effect of mad levanter.

We came in a mindless dawn to Mykonos,
There, in the first hot light upon the quay,
Smelled the fish-weed salt of wet warps
Drying and shrinking in a sun rolling
From a blind-white aphelion,
Burning its way to the high sky's blue:
Blue of sea and sky the only colour,
All else, the cat-in-pattens village,
Windmills on the hills, trim donkeys,
Caiques at anchor, even flowers
Seemed achromatic in that light
Which dwelt in purity of blue and white.
Such artless chastity was restful,
Making no demands, observed in clarity
As lambent as the place itself.

Nothing here touched a lively nerve,
No sudden revelation caught the breath,
The soft sea susurrated on the sand,
The warm wind wrapped the mind for sleep,
Seeping with the sun's creeping heat:
Coral and sponges dangled in the booths
And blue beads to avert the evil eye,
Doors opened on to opalescent caves
Where traders showed but did not press their wares:
And quiet everywhere, becalming thought.

Why should we not, among these Lotophagoi,

Eat honied fruit, and like Odysseus' men
Forget the needless restlessness
For knowledge, dangerous delight?
Why further test our sensibilities
When here men never struggled with the gods?
The gods had hardly noticed Mykonos:
Athens, Eleusis, were an aeon away,
To-morrow and to-morrow with the lotus seed . . .
The gods were unobservant? In like circumstance,
Odysseus dragged his men aboard in irons:
From Piraeus we had sailed south-east all night,
Now came a call to follow the sun's arc.

So we went to the ship, felt the spray
On our eyes, and the blown salt tasted,
Saw Delos isle lie low two miles away
And feared the gods watching the hours wasted
On sweet Mykonos, even now a dream:
A backward glance saw only bright white walls
Rising and falling in the dancing stream
Of wavelets bouncing wind-whipped crystal balls.
But Delos crouching in translucent haze
Burned in our eyes with mirrors of dull gold:
Nearer we tossed, the city came to gaze
Silently and blind. No one had told
Me no live thing would greet us at the quay,
But fallen temples staring avidly.

We stepped on shore, a hot wind from the sea
Came in a mad levanter, parchingly,
To whip the fine dust scathingly,
Slowing our feet intolerably
Till we came to a wide space
Ringed with sculptured stone and sat,
And others followed, saying that

Professor Simpkin told them of this place.
And as they spoke he came; not Tarragon,
But Simpkin with his sea-green eyes
Now half-closed in the treeless glare.
  'Now!' He began. 'I hope you all can hear:
  This is the market where ten thousand slaves,
  They say, could be disposed of in a day
  Around the second century B.C.,
  But that is late in Delos history,
  Riches and culture, and her virtue gone.
  Well may you ask how these could grow on
  Two square miles of granite, rock and sand,
  A barren islet in the Cyclades.
  You haven't? Well, then, hear and understand.

  Forget the slaves, such rich decline is dull,
  Of no significance, as most else is
  In my view since fourth century B.C.:
  Think of an island floating on these seas,
  And Leto seeking sanctuary
  To bear her child by Zeus, while Hera
  Drives her in jealous rage from rock to rock.
  The island, frightened on two scores,
  Dreads to offend the great god's angry wife,
  And fears, if Leto bears Apollo there,
  He'll soon despise so poor a place
  And stamp it down into the ocean depths
  To be reposeful dwelling for black seals,
  And elsewhere make his temple's wooded groves.
  But Leto swears it will be otherwise,
  And Zeus enchains the island motionless
  With crystal anchors to the deep sea's bed.

  Then Leto, hovering, at last alights
  Beside the palm you'll presently observe
  And there remains nine days in labour,

48

While Anatolian swans sing seven songs
High in the blue until Apollo's born,
But on that instant sweeping down
Flight after white flight, dipping wings;
The earth is flower-damasked
And all Delos from Mount Cynthus to the shore
Is bathed in gold.'
                          Professor Simpkin laughed
With fluttered hand. 'No poet, I:
'It's all in the Homeric Hymns,
I cribbed the language years ago at King's;
You buy the package in translation now
And learn far more than listening to me.

But let me tell you about Artemis,
That potent goddess and Apollo's twin
Born earlier on a rocky islet near,
Ortygia, which some call Rheneia,
Just across the way, while others argue
That Ortygia means simply quails,
The guise of Zeus and Leto when they loved.
The fact is Artemis was born instanter,
That's why at childbirth she's invoked,
For she so marvellously strong
Could help her mother bear Apollo,
Nine days younger than herself.

Be as it may, the cult of Delian
Apollo measures long as memory:
Homer himself sang here, with Hesiod
Competing in the panegyrics
At the great amphictyon.
Assemblies came from all the Cyclades,
The coasts of Asia and of Greece
To praise Apollo, spread Olympian fame,
And, as in other centres of the sort,

49

Besides the prayers and holocausts were games
And plays and music, and from these grew fairs
Until the tiny, barren isle became,
With the Athenians pulling all the strings,
The hub of riches in the trading world.
Here, too, the earliest school in marble
Kouroi in the Egyptian style, but naked,
From the hand of the first sculptor, Daedalus:
Yet with all secular pursuits and growth
The holy nature of the place remained;
Delos, above all, rejoiced Apollo,
And there to praise him the Ionians sailed
With wives and children, who in song
And dance and games displayed such skill
As made them seem, themselves, immortal.

In the Fifth Century B.C.
Athenian edict caused all tombs
To be removed, decreed as well
That persons who seemed like to die,
Or soon give birth, should also be transferred;
Which gave the Spartan cads excuse to say,
When asked for help, "There are no Delians".
In May each year to mark Apollo's birth
A sacred embassy from Athens came,
And till the ship returned no execution
Could profane the city.
So was the death of Socrates postponed,
And so the dialogue of Plato born
Narrating Phaedo's talk with Socrates
On death and immortality.

Then, later, as the shrine grew fat
So grew the markets richer still;
With Rome in the ascendent
Slaves sold in thousands, much vulgarity and show,

Till Mithridates, Eupator of Pontus,
Hating Rome, in 86 B.C.
Sacked Delos, took the women off
And killed the men.

                                    But time did not relent.'
In Simpkin's rhetoric a fresh pulsation
Gave warning of a studied peroration.
  'Two centuries on, a poet's soul is rent
To make the island grieve in words that went
Much like the earl of Arundel's Lament,
You may recall it; if you don't, I'll quote
At least a part to make it less remote:
"Bitter, bitter, oh to behould the grasse to growe
Where the walles of Walsingham so stately did shew"
Ah me, poor island that had sheltered homeless Leto,
Had I still drifted I should not be mourning so,
Desolate where the Greek World worshipped, bowing low,
Hera's avenged herself on me for Leto. Woe!
 ' "Sinne is wher our Ladie sate, heaven turned is to hel
Sathan sittes wher our Lord did swaye, Walsingham oh
                                    farewell".'

Professor Simpkin paused for brief applause,
A sound he loved, not always without cause.
  'One can't but find some similarities
With Dissolution of the Monasteries.
Thank you, now run along and look your fill
It's hot and creepy, so don't wait until
You're beat before returning to the ship,
We sail at drinking time's my final tip:
Though on this island it's then hardly dusk,
You'll know the hour by plants distilling musk.'

His voice was windswept as a seagull's cry
While I went quickly through the whispering grass,

And others wandered to a temple near
Steeped in the sun as dustily as bees:
I felt myself a mirage, dancing
In this man-made wilderness of stone,
A shadowy projection of the light
From the encircling glittering sea;

Whenever I caught sight of Tarragon,
His image was dissolved in earth or air,
Till, leaning by the place of Leto's shrine,
I saw his figure sharply, with arms raised
Towards a palm-tree in a dried-up lake.
Behind, between him and the dancing sea,
The avenue of Naxian lions stared
Wide-smiling, toothless, sly and sea-weathered
Smooth as seal sentries at this sacred place:
Lichened grey stone and marble among rocks
Joined gold and white with the sage-green lentisk;
Burned was the drooped flower of the parched cistus.

Maybe it was the wind or trick of ear,
I'm no Greek scholar, though I knew the sounds
Of the words carried on a sighing lull:
Tarragon sensed my being there and turned.
   'You also seek the heart of it?' he asked,
   Contemplatively watching my approach.
   'Did Simpkin tell you of the singing swans,
   Their home and why they came here specially?'
   'Yes, because here the twins were born,' I said.
   'Twins! Old as Hellas is that heresy.
   Odysseus, found by Nausicaa at dawn
   Cast by the sea upon her father's shore,
   Likened her figure to that palm there, said,
   "Only in Delos have I seen before
   Such grace." But note, Odysseus used his head
   And first compared her charms to Artemis,

Whom Homer calls Zeus daughter; Greeks believed
That story the old bard perpetuates.'
'It's what professor Simpkin said of her.'
'He did? A pity you should be misled.
His Christianity is masculine
And Protestant, he would have Artemis
Diminished, with Apollo for a twin
Who then surpasses her, her Mother too,
Divine Son of an Almighty Father:
He knows, no one than Simpkin better knows,
But certain vows, the cloth, inhibit him,
The clergy after all wear priestess' robes.

But he's a good man,' murmured Tarragon,
'Let's move a little further round this wall,
It's quieter from the wind, and there's no need
To trudge the streets of this demented town
To gaze at sanctuaries and porticoes:
The place is jammed with the theogony
That Hesiod and Homer here composed;
Apollo rules, so Dionysos too
Must counterpoise his temple
On Mount Cynthus' lower slopes,
Two phalloi on two columns, balls and all:
Old Man of the Sea, Glaukos, settled down
With Nereids and had an oracle,
Even the gods of Egypt had a precinct,
Isis and Serapis and others too,
As Lat, for Leto, brought by Ptolomies
Tainted with wealth and Hellenistic art;
The floating cross-roads meeting of two cults
That mirrors always man's duality,
Makes Delos fearful in its latent force,
Then culminates in crazy compromise.

This tale of twins, one by nine days delayed -

More like nine centuries!
Reading the story in Homeric Hymns
Leto in flight comes to Ortygia
And painlessly to Artemis gives birth,
Then, by the Delos palm-tree for nine days,
Slowly brings forth Apollo the young god,
While singing swans sweep by her sleepless head.

But there's Ortygia near Ephesos
Where Artemis the Great Earth-Goddess rules,
Leto, her mother, is just Lada. Just!
As though she were not womankind itself,
Who, in the aspect of Eurynome,
By Ophion laid the universal egg!
Swans were her sacred symbol, singing swans
From Anatolia; so come the parables
Of Helen's birth from Leda's swan-Zeus egg
And her consenting ravishment to Troy:
For Artemis was Anatolian,
Triple moon-goddess who went then to Crete,
And after centuries to Delos came
In the womb of the first Earth-Mother,
And here assisted at Apollo's birth.

Then comes the nub of it.
When after still more centuries
The gods supplanted the Great Goddess,
Homer placed Zeus firmly on his throne:
The matriarch lost to the patriarch,
Woman-creatress, served by sacrifice
Of puny kings, gave way to powerful gods.
The Delian Apollo still shared power
With Woman and her daughter, Artemis,
Who had not yet withdrawn their presence
As at Delphi where Apollo ruled.
Homer, although he backed Olympians,

Knew well this trio's Asian origins,
And made it, when the gods took sides, aid Trojans.
But Artemis had her revenge on men
For weakening her prime divinity . . .
Look there! That Greek girl guiding them; her hair
Is dark Callisto's, and her blackbird's eye:
Infinity is in her every step!'
He started up. 'They're coming now this way:
'The wind has madness in it, let us go.'
Professor Tarragon had jumped the wall.
    'Tell me,' I asked, 'why do you fear so much
    The colour of a Greek girl's eyes and hair?'
    'Artemis is a bear, is Callisto;
    No man has ever known her to be fair
    In deed or colour, yet she makes men burn
    And tremble while they feel the hot day cool,
    As did Hippolytus, Artemis' tool.'

I followed Tarragon, who, in a lope,
Made quickly for Mount Cynthus' lower slope,
And halting there, said, sinking on the sand,
    'Since this no doubt seems very strange to you,
    I'll tell a tale - no, nothing personal,
    Though close to all of us. You may not know
    That Fraser grew his Golden Bough from it,
    To pattern the profound philosophy
    Of man and nature's consanguinity.

    First there's Theseus of whom you'll soon learn more
    At Cnossos, where he kills the Minotaur
    And leaves with Ariadne then deserts her.
    Becoming king of Athens, he defeats
    The Amazons and weds Antiope
    Their queen, who's often called Hippolyte,
    Siring upon her young Hippolytus;

When presently she violently resents
His taking Ariadne's sister,
Phaedra, as another wife, he kills her.
You cannot think the gods were blind to this,
Especially the virgin Artemis.

So there's the stage all set for tragedy.
Hippolytus, a young man come of age,
Rules Troezen for his father: in that place
There is a shrine to Artemis
Whom Antiope had loved; now her son,
Taught by the centaur Cheiron how to hunt,
Adores the virgin huntress, spends his days
Racing with her through woods, scorns women
And remains as chaste as the fierce maid
Whose divinity he cherishes,
Not reckoning the fearful power of love.

Love's very goddess, Aphrodite,
Furious that Hippolytus should show such scorn,
Pricks his step-mother Phaedra with desire
When he comes garlanded to Eleusis:
Her passion then grows uncontrollable,
She follows him to Troezen, Athens,
Theseus absent fighting, or the gods knew where;
Her nurse (what should we do without
These nurses in the history of love?)
Persuades her to declare her heart's flame,
Praying Hippolytus reciprocate.
When true to form Hippolytus declines,
Failed Phaedra hangs herself, leaving a note
For Theseus that his son has ravished her.

Theseus, like Potiphar, believes her:
(Absurd, but natural, most husbands do,
Acceptance of such lies supports their pride)

And in his righteous rage he damns his son,
Calling upon Poseidon for revenge.
Hippolytus in flight from Athens
Drives for Troezen: in the narrow way
Between the Corinth and Saronic gulfs
A great wave crested with a roaring bull
Sweeps in and makes the horses mad;
For all his skill Hippolytus is doomed,
The chariot swerves, the beast pursuing screams,
When one rein catches in an olive branch,
The horses, filled with terror, throw him out
And tangled in the reins Hippolytus is dragged.
So dies the son of Hippolyte-Antiope,
But Artemis, that fertile angry virgin,
Gets Asclepius to revive him;
Zeus indignant at this resurrection
Sends Asclepius to Hades in his place.

From here the Latins take the story up,
Using their own barbaric names:
For Artemis, Diana; Zeus, Jupiter;
Artemis thinks first that Delos
Would suffice to hide Hippolytus,
But Zeus knows the place too well.
So she, whom now I'll call Diana,
Takes the young man enveloped in a cloud
To Nemi, where, by an Italian lake
Surrounded by deep groves of oak
There dwells the nymph Egeria.
And there forever dwells Hippolytus,
Changing his name to Virbius
Which means a man twice over.

The oak-grove then becomes Diana's shrine:
Horses are barred the sacred precincts,
And each year the appointed priest

Is darkly dispossessed, murdered
By his successor, who, entitled king,
Reigns till in turn his own blood stains the grove
Where oak sprouts mistletoe, the Golden Bough.
After some thousand years or more,
-Millennium's useful unit
In myth-history mélange –
The emperor Valerian condemns a Roman officer,
A Christian convert called Hippolytus,
To die by horses tearing him in pieces.'
Professor Tarragon's voice paused.
 'The macabre relevance of this increases
Since the saint's day's the same as Artemis's.'

'We seem.' I ventured, 'to have strayed from Delos.'
Sebastian Tarragon said, 'Trains of thought
'Should not be broken or there's loss
Of something while it's being sought;
So let me be: I have to find
First what it is that strains my mind.

Don't think I'm trying to escape reality
By duplicating visions as they spring
To my mind's eye: the proper test of sanity
Is deep suspicion of the gifts gods bring,
And yet acceptance of them, that's the point;
You mustn't put their noses out of joint.
Recall Callisto, Artemis' young maid,
Suspected Zeus, yet let herself be laid;
Condemned for this by Artemis to die,
Zeus then composed the Great Bear in the sky
To save her . . . Look! How her black hair flies
        the breeze,
As though already swept up there to freeze!
That's why they say the Brauron Artemis
Has little girls called arktoi dressed as bears;

But no one knows. A moon-white goddess, this,
Who man's first philosophic nimbus wears:
The bloody rites to speed fertility
Are overthrown by worship of virginity,
With paradox of woman in birth-throe
Crying with trust to Artemis-Leto.
By god, how terrible is woman! Dread,
Relentless nature governing her will,
The cool, white, sickle moon of maidenhead
Harnessing tides of passion's overspill.'

The girl still held his gaze: 'We are in thrall,' he said,
Then turned to deal with Delos history
As though delivering a practice talk
Before a mirror, rather overplayed:
His words like lambent, Pentecostal tongues
Burned visibly even in the hot light
Of the island's windy incandescence.
From time to time we moved, not with the sun
But as the group with which Callisto walked,
Turned from the lake to sanctuary of Bulls
With the horned altar that Apollo built
Where men had paced the stately Stork Dance maze:
More slowly trailed the thin procession now
To the house of Naxians, Leto's shrine,
Theatre, Precinct of Egyptian gods,
Mosaic of Dionysos: some climbed
To see the cave-shrine of Apollo, some
Panted to the very peak of Cynthus.
We, among ruins on the lower slopes,
Surveyed the whole city, saw the sun droop
From the blue roof of Ariadne's Naxos
In declining arc by Paros, seeming
To hang above Rheneia, westering
With wind still hot as frightened horses.

Eyes set upon Callisto, separate
Now from the flagging, polychrome pilgrims,
Tarragon spoke with parched voice.
                                    'Underrate
    'The primordial force, and all the hymns
    To gods, Apollo or Demeter, will
    Not save your reason or your world. Until
    You've grasped the double role of Artemis
    Divine, fertile and virgin, drunk the kiss
    That takes and gives alluring death and life,
    You'll also miss the underlying truth
    The Greeks found here at Delos without strife,
    That goddesses need gods to keep their youth.
    - Though vice-versa, dammit, is the bore
        That mortal men need goddesses still more.

    The tale of Phaedra and Hippolytus is
    Parable: Phaedra is Aphrodite,
    Lustful love, who tries to lure Adonis
    From Kore-Artemis the mighty,
    Huntress who both slays and is the giver
    Of all life in nature, cruel, tender;
    Virgin in name, but fertile she must be
    Since fertilizing works in sympathy.
    So there must be a male, a useful pawn
    Enjoying a brief rapture then dismissed:
    Another year revolves, a new spring born,
    Another lover in renewal kissed.

    Should we feel sorry,' the professor sighed,
    'For mortals caught by the passionless tide
    Of nature? A goddess' autumn choice
    To brood all winter, in the spring rejoice
    In the red stain on the anemone
    And mistletoe expended from the tree:
    She is fulfilled, at least till summer tires

And immortality the pawn requires.
The bloody springtime could be mine or yours,
But dare we hesitate to be the cause
Of pleasuring a goddess, though the price
Of immortality is sacrifice?'

His lips closed and his eyelids drooped;
Then all at once he rose, lean body stooped
Loose-jointed over me to bid me stay:
Then, throwing up his head, he was away.

Still I can feel that wind shaking me
With cold as I sweat, the dark sea
Deepening to wine flecked madly white
And hard-shadowed, but reflecting light
From the low burning sky, the rocks shining
And golden seed-pods all combining
With the ruined city's glinting grey
Dry bones, until I feel myself the prey
Of a dry fear the cause of which I sense
But cannot name. The silence is intense
Within the wind: the putt-putt of a boat's
Engine is unheard, the caique floats
Towards our ship, the few left on the quay
Wave, and a tall, black-maned one strides away
With swinging skirt to vanish in the dusk:
I smell the hour of earth's distillate musk.

'Where is professor Tarragon?'
'I do not know,' I said. 'Upon
My soul, I'm not his keeper. I might say
"And where have you been all the day?" '
There was no answer, which provoked me more.
'Perhaps you found my company a bore,'
I said. 'Perhaps,' was her reply.
I heard the sea's slap slipping by

As in the dark we turned our backs and slept
Fitfully, until the gods had wept
Had they not been so much amused
To see two mortals thus confused
By their Olympian jokes on life and death.

Then Eos woke us with her saffron breath,
Blushing to recall, as always, Delos
Where she seduced Orion. Sweet Eos'
Fingers stroke the thighs of night
And wedded to the dawn-wind bring the light;
So, when with Helios, she rode the morning,
My love smiled:
                'See! We've had our warning.
 'Unanswered questions bring ill-tempered fear,
No wonder our behaviour was queer.
Too many gods and ruins, blinding sun
And hot rocks crying with the wind may stun,
But, since evening and morning star are one,
Dawn never sets although the night's begun.'

VI

Forebodings at Samothrace - More Mysteries - Capering Cabiri
Sharp exchange between dons - The throat of Asia - Troy!

Now though the hours flow on continuously
The day has a strange light, the saffron breath
Of Eos blows more hot, the sea more dark
Becomes, moving as though a submerged hand
Sways powerfully and slow to cradle us,
Stirring a vague unease;
There are no shadows but a clear
Ponderous light on the deep-breathing sea;
The ship rides and slews laboriously
Swinging with the tide's set and crumpled wave,
Lured then repelled by the stupendous rock,
The mountain island, wooded Samothrace
Rising five thousand feet above the shore,
A crowned sea-monster, head in a red cloud
Smoking with the sun's heat imprisoned there.

Sebastian Tarragon said in my ear,
  'I doubt if we have anything to fear,
    But we'll soon know if we can land to-day,
    Depending what the gods have now in play;
    The war is going badly for the Greeks,
    Hector, his face like night with fury, seeks
    To burn the Argive hollow ships to hulks
    And save Troy while Achilles sulks:
    But with the gods so evenly divided
    The war will only be decided
    When Zeus, who usually backs Trojans,

Wearies of it. Another god then churns
The brew! '

On the high peak the sky-wind blew
The parting mists, and from them grew
A great head, turned south-east to stare
Across the sea to Troy, teeth bare
To grit the dust of battle there.
   'My God!' said Tarragon, 'From there he sees
The whole of Ida. If the Achaeans flee,
- I say Achaean, Argive; Homer did,
To cover Greeks with one poetic lid -
Poseidon, see his sulky stare,
Will stride to his sea palace where
Await his chariot and golden steeds,
Resources submarine and all he needs
With which to reach the failing Grecian side,
Give it new heart and turn the battle's tide
On furious Hector, Priam's son.'
He paused: 'Would that this war were done,
'And you, fair Hector, held Andromache
Whose white arms rock your son contentedly.
Poseidon's leaving Samothrace will make
The waves more . . . Look!' He seized my arm.
                    'Look, look, his wake!'

The great sea-beasts with gambols reverential
Rushed to salute their monarch existential;
The sea itself, delighted at his passing,
Opened an avenue with curved sides massing
On either hand to keep his axle dry
While gold-maned horses made his chariot fly!

The sun-pierced spray flew in a crystal shower,
The sound of flippers clapping on the hull
Sea-slapping in enthusiastic praise

64

Merged in Tarragon's transcendent vision.
Then when the spindrift passed, it seemed a door,
High, secret, in a wall surrounding me
Had been flung open and as sudden closed:
The mist was once more formless on the peak,
No sigh of wind disturbed the wooded sides,
But sea-swell soft as silken sleep still swayed
The ship on smooth slopes rolling to the shore.

No boat could land us on those hilly waves,
So we lay lulled by sunlight, undulant,
Feeling the deck's pressure and withdrawal
While the tale of the unvisited isle sang
In Tarragon's and Simpkin's antiphon.
We listened, dozed, then woke again to see
Pillars like bleached trunks in the Sacred Grove,
A cleft with river running to the sea
That held the ruins of Anaktoron,
The Temenos, Hieron and Altar,
The fountain, where theatre crowds once saw,
Outlined against the deep Aegean sky,
The sublime winged niké on her ship's prow.

All there to see at lazy turn of head,
The stones, white goats among the trees and sheep
Nibbling their way to the blue water's edge;
So close, but hardly comprehensible,
As shrouded as the island's Mysteries,
Sacred and more secret than Eleusis,
The only script that might interpret them
Done by a Pelasgian who used
Greek Characters to spell his arcane words,
The oldest of archaic schoolboy jokes.

'First, there was the Great Mother of the Rocks,
With Kadmilos a secondary god,

65

Not unimportant though since he begot
The Cabiri, the twin divinities,
Gods of Fertility, the basic cult.
Inside the All-Holiest, the temple
Where the Hieron was built, a brother
To these two was worshipped: what relation
To the Great Mother he possessed was hid,
But it was said the twins had murdered him,
Burying his head at Mount Olympus.
I won't pursue this hare,' said Simpkin, 'else,
What with the Corybantes, Cybeles
And parsley sprung from the killed brother's blood
And so taboo, you're bound to get confused.

On either side the temple's entrance stood
Twin phallic statues of the Greek god, Hermes,
Or so the Greeks thought, though in fact the god
Was Asian with a score of names
All meaning he inspired fertility;
He was wrought always by Pelasgians
With erect phallus, and Athenians
Were the first Greeks to copy this
From the Samothracian Mysteries.
When, some seven centuries before Christ,
Greeks came upon the old performances
Practised from time beyond all memory,
They moderated them to suit their gods,
Retaining the procreant Mystery
But giving to the gods Olympian names
And carrying on the rites less rudely.
Mother of the Rocks became Demeter,
Kadmilos, her husband-son, Greek Hermes,
Cabiri became Dioscuri, sons
Of Zeus by Leda, Caster and Polydeuces,
Twin gods invoked by sailors, which is why
Orpheus, pupil of the Cabiri,

Had brought the Argonauts to Samothrace . . .'

'Then slow but surely,' took up Tarragon,
'The Mysteries became more spiritual:
Those who came to be initiated
Here in Samothrace came for an answer
To the deep question of man's entity,
The why, the whence and whither of his life,
How to relate his actions to his thought,
His sight and what his hearing tells him.
In this they went much further than Eleusis,
Perhaps because they were far more remote;
In spite of fame and patronage of kings
They did not get mixed up in politics.'

'Say, rather more or less,' Simpkin observed.

'You needn't think because of this,' said Tarragon,
'Greeks made the Mysteries more intellectual:
Here in Samothrace to make confession,
Seek a moral good and feel the better for it,
Was an impulse of the heart not mind.
Spiritual drifting from the drómenon
Still kept the ritual to suggest
That learning the inward from the outward
Is more exciting for the soul
Than learning from the inward, inwardly.
I much enjoy this aspect of the Greeks:
It must have been a lovely place to live.'
'Oh, pish!' said Simpkin. 'Romans were more practical,
And saw the propaganda value of the place,
By claiming their descent from Trojan Aeneas
Who took the peneates from Samothrace;
Aeneas, descendant of that Dardanus,
Who, when the first flood burst the Hellespont,
Crossed to Asian mount Ida on a raft.'

The ship lurched: Tarragon laughed soft.
  'Such talk is dangerous: the shore's too close
  Where Corybantes beat upon their shields
  In Cnossian dance, with forests joining in,
  And bears and lions roaring joy
  And capering Cabiri in madness sane:
  The bird of morning cuts the air with cries.
  You hear it? No? That man who enters
  Wonderfully dressed, twanging his cither with a quill,
  Sings the Great Mysteries as random as a blind man
  Sings of what he sees, who with his inward eye
  Knows what he cannot clearly tell: so he cries
  On the offspring of great Rhea, of Zeus, Cronos:
  "O Attis, whom Assyrians call Adonis
  Thrice-desired, and Egypt call Osiris,
  The celestial horn of crescent moon,
   And Samothracians name Adam,
   Greeks, wisdom, and Haemonians, Corybas;
  Phrygians sometimes Papas, sometimes corpse,
  Or god or fruitless or the goatherd,
  Reaped ear of green corn
  Or the piper, man,
  Who was begot by fruitful Amygdalus,
  Father of the Universe:
  Here, then is Attis multiform . . ."
  Make Roman sense of that rhapsodic hymn!'

Simpkin ignored his colleague's parting thrust,
Which from a fellow-don he felt unjust.
  'I'll quote you Philostratus,' Simpkin said,
  'He has an apt reflection on this head:
  "If about everything we cannot hold
  Our tongues, at any rate be not so bold
  As to break silence on such things as these,
  Of which our ignorance can hardly please."

As I was saying,' he resumed, 'Dardanus,
Zeus' son, reached Asia near the Hellespont,
Hence Dardanelles, the story's told by Aeneas
When boasting to Achilles of his pedigree:
The best tale of the lot is of Dardanus' son,
Who has three thousand mares whose beauty so seduced
The North Wind that he, Boreas, became
A stallion choosing twelve mares for his love;
The twelve foals he engendered were so fleet
Their hooves brushed harmlessly the standing corn,
And when they frolicked by the sea
Faster than foam-flecks skimmed the crests.'
Simpkin received a gentle laugh for this,
And, gratified, said,

                              'Be that as it may,
'Dardanus' son's son gave the Troad name,
And his son, Ilus, built the city Troy:
Apollo told him to pursue a cow
And where the cow lay down construct his walls,
As later did Saint Cuthbert's followers
Whose Christian god brought them to Durham
Led by a cow who rested on a hill,
A hill more fortunate than doomed Ate
Where nine successive Troys . . .'

And then I dozed; the ship swung on her way,
Loosed from her moorings on an oily swell
To sail south-eastwards, Imbros to starboard,
And the coast of Asia . . . lovely Asia . . .

Soon the ship trembled with an inner urge,
Striving with all the streams of Russia
Pouring through the Hellespont
From Marmora, Bosphorus and Euxine,
Where lay Colchis and its Golden Fleece,
The narrow throat of Asia spouting life

Scintillant, sinister and swirling.
Here Leander swam on short summer nights
From Abydos to Hero in her tower
Near Sestos, where she served the goddess
As her priestess in the day, with darkness
Practised what she'd learned of Aphrodite
With Leander, guided by her torch,
Until, alas, a tragic winter's night
Blew out the light, and, in grey morning's sight,
Desolate Hero plunged into the sea
That swirling thirstily had drowned her love.
So, from the moment in eternity
When Helle slipped from the Winged Golden Ram,
To the white monuments that stud the cliffs
Above the beaches of Gallipoli,
Death has too much prevailed, inopportune,
Wrought on the innocent by arrogance
And the fierce serpent waters.

'You see,' said Simpkin, 'how the calm sea writhes
With continual whirlpools, laying, as scythes
Do with the mown grass, succeeding arcs
Whorled on the surface; these are the marks
Of the water's power that made Troy great,
With oil, jade, cinnabar and iron freight:
Few cargoes under sail could force this strait,
With pirates added to the current's sleight;
So on that hill there three miles from the mouth
Rose Troy to guard trans-shipment by the south
Route overland, to join the sea once more
At Lampsachos not far from Marmora -
The centre of the cult of Priapus,
Who, ithyphallic, brings *in urbe, rus:*
Item to this, Troy had two resources,
Weaving and a splendid breed of horses,

70

Five thousand years ago the first Troy grew.
Three thousand since king Priam's town was new,
About a thousand since all passed from view
With no sound but an errant sea-bird's mew:
Now only nibbling goats in windblown mists
Mimic the talk of archaeologists.'

Alike to whirlpools on the Hellespont
Are the concentric circles of Troy's walls
Upon the airy hill of Hissarlik,
Spreading their ripples where each city grew;
Complexity of convoluting lines,
A battlemented chaos of man's work
On hummocks covered with long, thin, pale grass
On which the wind plays ever a lament
Beneath the ravishing Levantine sky.

Coming from Kannakale by the sea
We sat at eve above the Scaean Gate,
Feeling the day's heat rising from the plain:
Unseen were Scamander and Simois
Where lotus grow, and galingale and reeds,
Scamander of the Deep Silver Eddies
Whose lovely channels, choked with Trojan dead,
Rose in wild spate against Achilles . . .
A timeless quiet falls upon the place:
The rest all gone, we stay, my love and I,
Callisto and fleet-footed Tarragon,
Hearing the long grass flute above the stones,
The whispering swift sandals on the sand,
And our hot pulse-beats like the clash of bronze.

'They have been here nine years,' Tarragon said.
'Each month among the Greek and Trojan dead

More noble names appear. Patroclus, slain
By Hector, tears Achilles from his vain
Sulking, and to-morrow . . . But there's no then
And now: time's journey has no instant "When";
Already, brute Achilles in his rage
Has donned Haephaestos' armour, of a gauge
No man, save the gods help, can penetrate;
See how the Trojans pour back through the Gate!'

Below the hill the plain runs to the sea
And the Achaean beaked ships' thousand masts:
Near to their tents, Patroclus' burial mound
Smokes faintly as the funeral games begin,
Giving the dying sun a pyre-like glow.
The tragedy of Troy is in full flood:
I shake beneath an overwhelming weight.
They have closed the Gate! Outside stands Hector
Facing alone the Greeks whose sloping shields
Come steadily. A sharp light strikes my eye,
Like to that autumn star in evening skies
They call Orion's Dog; this evil star,
Achilles' bronze now flashing on the plain,
Rivals the setting sun. I turn my head,
Seeking in Tarragon some saving sense:
Besides me stands loved Hecabe, none else.
    'Hector!' I cry. 'Hector, my son! Within the walls
    Is safety, and your bravery can yet save Troy.
    Have pity! There you court defeat and death.'
    And 'Oh, my darling boy!' Weeps Hecabe.

But our voices are swept by the hot wind:
Hector is firm, watching with a snake's eye
Glittering the foe, weighing in his thoughts
To fight or parley, knowing he must fight.
Only the gods know how his fear mounts,
As wild Achilles in his savage pride

Bears blazing down on him in burnished bronze.
Then Hector turns; and, like a shrieking hawk
Swoops on a dove, Achilles darts at him:
By the walls they race, horse-taming Hector
And Achilles fleetest of all runners,
But neither gains. In the nightmare silence
Of the city and the watching armies
I can hear the whispering of the gods.

Three times the racers have encircled Troy,
Passing the cart-tracks and the ripe fig-tree,
The stone wash-troughs, the cool and lovely springs
All so beloved before the Achaeans came.
At last they halt, facing with grinning masks;
Hector sees by his side Deiphobus,
Disguised Athene swearing brotherhood,
But, when the first long-shadowed spears are cast
And Hector calls his brother for the next,
No one is there. By this divine deceit
He knows the gods have beckoned him to death.

Under the deep, tender dome of evening
I stare, knowing I have seen this before.
Below me Hector and Achilles crouch;
I sweat and tremble, reaching searchingly
To find Hecabe, and, as I touch her,
Hector springs. But, swifter than Hector's sword,
Achilles' lance drives at his armour's chink
Where neck meets shoulder, piercing him.

'My son, my son! They have slit the tendons
Of your nimble feet and tied them with strips
To Achilles' chariot. The horses
Bound forward and your head drags in the dust.'

Above the lamentation of my voice

A great cry sounds and I am thrust aside:
Tall dark Andromache has heard the shouts
And with foreboding rushes from her house,
Now from the battlements she sees her prince
Pulled by the horses on the plain of Troy.

The sun sets swiftly in a purple mist,
The camp fires of the Greeks come out at last
Reflecting the impassive firmament.
Hecabe weeps, Andromache is dumb,
Grieving too terribly for tears or words.
In some chamber - or is it in my head? -
Helen and Paris quarrel: ten long years
And still they love and bicker to our shame,
Their wretched voices counterpoint Troy's death.
And I? What is there left for me to do?

I must go down through the whispering grass,
Over the grey, stumbling rocks to find my son;
All that was left for me of Troy is gone,
If I must die, I will die in this search,
That he be given proper burial
For Hecabe's and Andromache's sake.
I am going out by the southern gate,
It is easier there for an old man
And for the wagon and rich gifts I take
In ransom to the killer of my son.
This wind that I've so often cursed,
Tearing the grass, may hide the creaking cart;
And this young-bearded man in gold sandals
Appearing suddenly from the dark night
Will lead me through the sleeping Grecian lines.

I have come to the hut of Achilles,
He has eaten and drunk and sits scowling:
I must be humble, banish kingly pride

And kiss this barbarian's bloody hands;
For Hecabe's and Andromache's sake
I abase my great body, grasp his knees,
And beg him by his father's memory
To grant me what he would have wished for him,
The body of my son for burial.
The sound of lamentation fills the hut.

Then it is done, and an end to weeping,
Achilles fears to sin against the gods
Without whose help I had not come to him;
He weeps for his father and Patroclus.
I must not trust a Greek who makes a gift
Even of my son's body: I must go.
Already dawn dusts the plain with saffron
As Hermes leads my horses through the ford,
And the long shadows shrink towards the east
Where towered Ilium awaits the dead.

My eyes are tired, and I see mounds not towers.
I hear your scream, my fey child, Cassandra:
    'Trojans! Women of Troy! Welcome Hector
    As you did when he returned from battle!'
Tall dark Andromache of the white arms
Holds my son's head between her supple hands.
    'Too young!' she moans, 'to leave me with our son.
    Why did you not die in your bed, with arms
    Outstretched and words to treasure with my tears?'
And Hecabe my wife makes her lament:
    'Nothing Achilles did has spoiled your youth;
    You are as dew, one whom Apollo's
    Silver Bow has slain with gentle darts.'

They have lit the pyre by the Gate; the heat
Is blown to me by the all-searching wind
In the glare of the eye-burning sunset:

75

F

Sunrise to sunset, time's passage blinds me.
Now the sun's ball is altogether gone;
Seawards, the mole-black dunes are rimmed with fire,
The blue infinity of space and time
Pales to an exquisite transparency:
Pennants of dry grass flutter on the mounds,
And through the bushy battlements wind sweeps;
Always this madness of wind whispering,
Questioning, rising and fading, rising
But never answering, whispering . . .

The white ship idled on the inland sea:
   'Helen, of course, was held for her adultery
   In Egypt,' Simpkin said. 'She never was in Troy.'
The cool, don's voice came out to me, where leaning
On the rail I heard still the dry wind keening.
   'You only have to read Herodotus, Book Two,
   Where he sets out what is self-evident and true,
   To see that Trojans, grasping the event,
   Would have surrendered Helen sans consent
   Of Paris, if they'd had her; Trojans were no fools
   Who'ld land themselves in self-destruction as the tools
   Of a young prince's lust. The trouble was no Greek
   Believed them when they vowed they hadn't got her.
                           "Seek,"
   They said, "All Troy, for her and stolen treasure."
   "If there, you can have both with brimming measure."
   The Greeks thought this a frivolous reply,
   And one with which they could not well comply.
   The siege of Troy then ran its bloody course
   Till sharply ended by the Wooden Horse:
   To Egypt Menelaus went hot-foot
   And found in Memphis Helen and the loot.

The questionable point of why the Greeks refused
To test the Trojan's word, Herodotus excused

On grounds they were inspired by Providence
To disbelieve, and spurn it as pretence,
So that Troy's downfall might make evident
That sin brings down on man God's punishment.
My own view is, that though I will go far
For Helen-Paris as the cause of war,
It mainly gave the very good excuse
Required by Agamemnon to reduce
Control by Troy of all that Black Sea trade,
The Gorgeous East in fee, you know, the Chinese jade
                                   . . .'

Sad strain of warp, salt ripple on the hull:
A voice from darkness said, 'There is no line
  'Where myth concludes and history begins;
The one is poetry, the other prose,
Without the first the second has no life,
And each feeds each to grow a hybrid tree.
Such tragedies as Troy's are much alike;
They were before the Curse of Atreus,
Beginning when the Garden's gate was closed
By Cherubims with flaming swords on guard.
How long has their ignoble course to run?
Ah, me!
Would that this war were done,
And you, fair Hector, held Andromache,
Whose white arms rock your son contentedly!'

ANNODOMINICAL INTERLUDE IN BYZANTIUM

Coming from a world of infinite translucence
Where all things and beings have their own radiance,
To a world made real only by the sunlight
It objectively reflects, I am in doubt, as might
A dweller in the fishy deep be when he leaves
His element and in a rusty sun perceives
His scales that shimmered from a light within grow dim,
And fears the new light lacks reality for him.

Between swirled, leaden water and clear, dawn-blue skies,
The needle minarets and bowls of mosques arise
Unimaginable, yet visible and still,
Reflecting dawn's first flush upon Byzantium's hill
From a sun waking, and, as a mullet dying
Loses the deep red glitter of his scales, fading
To an intense sandy-pink. No less delicate,
Exquisite and unworldly is the intricate
Weaving of the lost souls of the dark Bosphorus,
Shearwaters skimming with flashes of phosphorous
From their white underparts as they veer aimlessly,
Like Paolo and Francesca, always restlessly,
Al vento esser leggieri, ceaselessly.

Those minarets and domes, countless in silhouette,
Prick and raise taut-drawn bows upon the sky they fret
In a cool pattern; seemingly the ship floats still,
While the swift stream unrolls dissolving views, until
We turn near Buyuk Dere, where the channel curls,
And see how the black water of the Euxine swirls

Down upon us. So I drift backward on its flood
Towards Hellenic seas, the sky reflecting blood
From the rich, ancient surface of the Golden Horn
Where Christians slew Christians, ignoring the Child born,
Wasting Byzantine loveliness He had inspired,
Until the Turks caught them, quarrelsome and tired,
And slew them also unreservedly, in spate
Entering by an open, though unpurposed, gate.
As I come, the evanescent dawn light's vision
Flies from the hot-risen, searching sun's precision.

The sun climbs implacably the pale firmament;
I gasp the humid air inside the stifling tent
Of sky that holds the dust and clamour of the town,
Where choking chicken's feathers float like thistledown.
Byzantium, Constantinople, Istanbul,
Greek Byzas, Christian Constantine and Oriental:
Here it must stand, declared the Delphic Oracle,
Secure and beautiful and hierarchical.

What's gone is gone; the future is preventable,
Or may be, if man only would be sensible:
So to look backward with regret on what has been
Has not the tantalising fear of things foreseen,
As I feel here, rising from my illumined deep
To see in harsh, prophetic light the long years creep
Over Byzantine hills from seven centuries
Before Christ came. Why should Darius Hystaspes
Destroy this place? Is his great empire not enough?
When his son Xerxes, passionate for the stuff
Of conquest, is repulsed, why must returning Greeks
Renew their feud with Greeks? Wherever my mind seeks
A mitigating cause, appears men's silliness
To turn a lovely world into a wilderness.
Hands wonder at the sculpture and the frescoed wall,

Minds seek the libraries . . . Smoke rises from the fall
Of the city. Latin, Crusader, Ottoman,
Friend, ally, foe, all show themselves barbarian.
What few Byzantine glories now remain
Are scattered as gale-seeded flowers stain
A stubbled field far from the Golden Horn.
Still on the Turkish flag and coins is borne
The crescent of moon-goddess Hecate who paved
The sea with light, and from the Macedonians saved
The city. Ritualist Byzantines at least
Preserved the manuscripts of Greece for us to feast
On: but for them we should not know Euripides,
Plato, Pindar, Aeschylus, Aristophanes,
To name a few: yet, if *we* disappear to-night,
The little more we've learned of radiating light
Is likely to be no loss to posterity;
The living left will have to start society
At chapter eight of Genesis, without regrets,
If God his rainbow covenant forgets,
And write another Testament, of loving kind
And wisdom where the blind no longer lead the blind.

I hope.

Again the warm Aegean murmurs in my ears,
Drowning my maudlin and unnecessary tears.
Leaving a world made real by history's light,
- Objective sun! - the doubts I had about my sight
Are gone: seeing things lit with their own radiance,
I swim into a world of infinite translucence.

VII

Sapphics - Blind old man of Chios - Vision of Seljuk - Tarragon's
discourse at Ephesos on Artemis, the Logos and much else - Further
dispute between dons - Callisto asserts primacy of woman - A
crescent smile.

I was rolling happily in the water,
Thinking of strophes composed in sapphic metre:
The dawn made each succeeding thought seem sweeter,
Though embryonic.
Bright the sky as I rose up like a porpoise,
Hoping the sun ascending behind Lesbos
Might help my verse, as Sappho's to Alkaios,
With fair adonic.

But to drift back that far, and try to speak
In sapphics suited to Aeolians
Seven centuries before our own two thousand years,
Is too disturbing; also false. I do not seek
To rival Sappho's friend, Alkaios,
Who wrote an ode to say shame held him
From the things he wished to tell: to which
She very properly replied, had his desire
Been good, shame would have neither touched his eyes
Nor quenched his words.
                            They say she sang her verse
In Mixo-Lydian mode invented by herself;
Her strange, sweet-smiling songs' supremacy
Sprang from their symmetry of sound and sense.
This had been pre-determined when the lyre
And head of Orpheus floated here from Thrace,

After the Maenads of Dionysos
Had torn him limb from limb: his head enshrined,
His lyre was made a constellation
To maintain the music of the spheres.

So passed dark Lesbos red-rimmed in the dawn,
And presently, as hours drift easily,
There floats to starboard Chios, island of figs,
White wine, Homer and the Homeridae:
    ' "The blind old man of Chios' rocky isle," '
I hear the voice of Simpkin quote, then doze,
Listening, as a blind man in the market-place
Sees with an inward eye the story told,
Or, by a window on hot summer days,
A child hears with a still, attentive face
His master teaching him his history,
While in his mind quite separately
Work other thoughts and visions, of the trees,
Of birds, of mermaids, unicorns and bees,
Which do not quite exclude the words he hears,
And blending make more sense than first appears.

Yet, with the voice and silky slip of sea
To soothe, my mind recalls uneasily
That day on Delos, the dry fear I felt,
And how the dusk-distillèd musk had smelt:
    'Most Chians were Euboeans,' Simpkin said.
And how, there, Tarragon's unruly head
With sensuous erudition followed
The dark, white-armed Callisto where she led
Her curious flock among the ruins.
    'But in Ephesos,' said Simpkin, 'there begins
    A deeper understanding of the terror
    Artemis inspired in girls whose error
    Lost them their virginity. Amazons
    Are her priestesses, and so do not have sons,

Save through some custom that is bye-the-bye,
    No doubt our Tarragon will tell you why. . . '
The cradling waves and overpowering light
At last transport me: I bestride an arch,
An arc of rainbow light from Ephesos
That spans to Delos where it came to earth,
Thence I have climbed, and halfway saw Troy's flood
Tumbling its dead beneath this springing bridge,
Which God, in a promise half-fulfilled,
Told Noah he would set here in the cloud,
A rainbow to remind Him of his vow
That never more would waters flood the earth,
Nor he, again, smite every living thing.
And then it seems this arch down which I slide
Was set by many-breasted Artemis,
Who, doubtful of such talk, set her own bow
Before this savage God's forgetful eye.
From a deep sky I hear his pompous voice:
    'While earth remaineth there shall never cease
    Summer and winter, burning heat and cold,
    Seed-time and harvest with its sure increase,
    These shall not cease, although the world grow old.'

                            'If I may be so bold,'
                Said Simpkin, 'it is time you stirred.
            'We're landing where the east and west con-
                                            curred.'

We wove inland up from Kusadasi by the sea
To Seljuk on a hill; three camels swaggered past us,
Loaded, insolent in their indifference, ageless
As the self-same beasts who bore the Virgin Mary
In her old age here with the Evangelist.
    'Ayassoluk this place was called, till shortened,'
    Simpkin said. 'Corruption of St. John Theologos,
    'The title of Justinian's grand basilica

In which we stand.' He gaily waved his tendril hand;
'A while ago few traces could be seen;
Ibn Batuta saw it whole in 1333,
And afterwards, oblivion: now, though the stones
And marbles dug and partly shaped to the first plan
Look somewhat like Lotts Bricks, this blazing sun
Can cook the imagination to perceive
Its ancient grandeur, with six cupolas,
Rich capitals and monogram of Theodora
And her emperor who knew about Byzantine art.

I daresay you may wonder why we're here:'
He paused, bare-headed in the incandescent heat.
  'Look round you from this flattened Turkish hill
At the parched slopes gilt with summer seed-pods,
Feel, but, I beg you, do not swoon at autumn's breath
That makes the mountains bluer and the stones more white:
See there below, the mosque of Isa Bey
Stands with a broken minaret and not far off
A Roman aqueduct with colonies of storks,
Above, a Turkish fortress once Byzantium's:
Look down! Between us and the shrinking sea
Are green mounds in a marsh. Can you discern
The rubble of a Wonder of the World
Seven times rebuilt, now swallowed by the swamp?
There stood the temple of great Artemis,
The virgin mother-goddess, Queen of Heaven.

The self-same holy contradiction once
Brought thousands to this fine basilica:
So from this hilltop you can contemplate
A pregnant continuity of faith;
To southward, over that first range of hills,
There is a little church they say contains
The last house where the Virgin Mary lived,
And in an olive grove her statue stands.'

Then quiet lay while Simpkin stroked his nose,
Preparing for his controversial close.
    'It was not very long ago occurred
    A vision to a lady, who, much stirred
    By dreaming of the Blessed Virgin's home,
    Despatched two learned scholar friends to comb
    This countryside by following the course
    Of what she'd dreamed. Surprised, they found the source
    Was where, since ages immemorial,
    The people there still held spring festival;
    To speed fertility their rites were danced
    In March upon the very day, it chanced,
    Christians celebrate Annunciation;
    By an olive tree, they made oblation
    To the White Goddess: if you dare to rove,
    You'll find the Virgin's statue in the grove.
    But now we'll off to Ephesos, and note,
    You'll see it clearer for this anecdote.'

The sprawled city lies in burrowed quiet
Among the hills, its colonnaded ways
Retain no echo of our shuffling feet,
Sound is still-born where half-discovered streets
Slide languidly between their broken walls
Like lava streams that spread on to the plain,
With temples, houses and gymnasia,
A little brothel near the library,
Odeion, Prytaneion, Agora
To serve the Asian metropolis.
Its Lydian and Ionian past
Deep buried beneath Graeco-Roman stone,
The city remains solemn in disuse:
On the Arcadian Way six chariots
Abreast could drive on pavements to the port
Of Cayster river and the sea, where ships
From all the waters of the ancient world

85

Came trading for the riches of the East.
The pavement ends, swamp swallows up the quays,
The distant sea glints unrepentently.

Still gazing down this straight, triumphal way,
Inviting to its plays the traveller,
The great theatre seeks for sunset seas.
  'Seats for twenty thousand shouting patrons,
  Where the silversmiths came in their aprons,'
  Simpkin said. 'Not horribly barocco
  'Like the rest: Greek-Roman drives me loco.
  I'm a purist. Come, I've done my bit to-day;
  Let's hear what Tarragon has got to say.'

Tarragon leans on the thumele,
That once had been the altar of a god,
There in the centre of the orchestra,
Chin on hand, staring at the sandy floor.
Slowly he lifts his head; tier above tier
His eyes move upward, till they meet the blue
Behind the topmost range of stone-cut seats
Of the vertiginously high theatron.
  'Great is Diana of the Ephesians!'
His words soft-spoken bring reply
From a high seat against the sky:
  'Whom all Asia and the world worshippeth.'

  'You hear? There was no need for them to shout,'
  Said Tarragon. 'They knew about
  'Acoustics, but they were inflamed
  By Paul; Demetrius cannot be blamed
  For stirring silversmiths to save their trade
  In shrines and holy statuettes they'd made
  For centuries. It's also not amiss
  To say that this Diana, namely Artemis,

A thousand years before Paul came
Had symbolised the living flame
Of life that fertilized the earth,
As did the Resurrection and the Virgin Birth
With much more subtlety expressed by Paul.
In essence men's faiths differ little if at all;
The rationalists and new psychology
Repeat what is old hat to Greek theology.
But, to round off this piece of history,
The town-clerk came: "There is no mystery
"In who is worshipped here in Ephesus,"
He said, "therefore no reason for this fuss.
"If there's a case you think you ought
To bring, you've got the law, the court:
If not, you're laying up a store
Of trouble with this day's uproar.
Do nothing rashly, go away:
This sort of nonsense doesn't pay." '

I saw Callisto, the dark, white-armed one,
Watch him with damson eyes. Spring to autumn
As the cruise-ships sailed into the bays,
She strode intuitively her ruins:
Soon with the season's end she would be gone
To Ithaca - her birth-place, so she said,
Though Tarragon said Brauron was more apt
Which had its source in Anatolian hills.
Her high-boned, guarded face stared vigilant,
Till, all at once, her eyes projected light
Like a spear-thrust, meeting his turned on her.

Tarragon said sharply,
    'Amazons were the founders of this place,
    By no means mythological, a race
    Of people ruled by matriarchy,
    Whom the Greeks, who came with patriarchy,

Made legendary to suit their game,
Adapting gods but with a change of name.
First, understand, the goddess worshipped here
Is old as time, when men were mere
Accessories before the fact of birth,
Begetters: women were the power on earth.
Such were the people of the Caucasus,
At least one must conjecture it was thus,
Since Hittites, when they first descended,
Brought here a goddess who was blended
Of Astarte, Atargatis and Semïramis,
Possessing the main qualities of Artemis;
Here was the fish and Ascalon's sacred dove,
The hind of Artemis, the antelope of love,
Which, the earth lacking, cannot flower to seed
And grow again, fulfilling the fierce need
Of all creation for the act each spring
Of procreation. Thus can woman bring
In autumn harvest and regenerated earth
From a year dying at its own re-birth:
From this derives the emblem of the bee
At Ephesos; the queen, rising from the tree
To meet the drone, mates with him in the skies;
He dies, and with his seed she multiplies.

A very goddess to inspire Ionians
Who'd fled Greece from the desolating Dorians:
From tenth to seventh century B.C. there grows
Here, in her fertile shadow, what the west knows
As the first flowering of philosophy.
"O se del mezzo cerchio far si puote
Triangol si, ch'un retto non avesse."
Abstract geometry's in Paradiso
While Dante meets the author still in Limbo;
He, Thales, is the first in multiplicity
To seek a single cause and driving unity:

Anáximander and Anaximenes,
Whose two great generations follow these
'Researches, tempered Hylozoism
Without evolving into mysticism . . .'

'He'll lose 'em,' whispered Simpkin with a yawn.
'You can't excite 'em with this kind of corn.'

'In other words, the theory that life
Is just part of matter, rife with life,
Threw out a life-line to the wider thought:
The very nature of the force they sought.

You think I'm wandering, but I'm not,'
Said Tarragon. 'If you come here you've got
To know the essence of the place you see,
Or else, for all I care, you ought to be
In Hampstead, Sussex, Boston or the Shires,
Not where the very burning dust inspires
To contemplation of the life of man,
The universe, his place in it, the span
Of centuries, joy, terror in his lot:
Move sideways to the shade if you're too hot.

Hard on their heels there came Heraclitus
The regal-hieratic basileus,
So aristocratic in his thought and speech,
Few men, even philosophers, could reach
The dark profundity, the blinding heights
To which his mind attained, setting its sights
On obscure nature's fundamental fact,
Namely, there's only the continuous act
That is Becoming, no estate of Being:
Everything is and yet is not, seeing
The only universal fact is change,
Eternal flux with an aesthetic range.

No immortality lies in a rose,
The truth of beauty but an instant knows:
So he arrives at relativity,
With harmony in multiplicity.

He sees in fire the clear embodiment
Of the Becoming, the active element
From which all things, the very soul evolved,
And into which are finally resolved:
This fire itself is the divine process
Harmonised in universal Logos,
Logos, reason, loosening the tension
From which life springs, keeping it in motion.

You have to die if you're to be reborn:
Mark how from Nature-Goddess and reaped corn
And bees of Artemis comes flowing
Creative growth of deep self-knowing,
One with knowledge of the Logos,
Reason universal out of chaos:
"In the beginning was the Word
The Word was with God and the Word was God."

See how it all leads naturally to John?
Wait now, five hundred years run on
Between Heraclitus and Philo,
The Greek-Jew of Alexandria, who
Gave divine dynamic to the Logos,
Not a mere immanence in the Cosmos:
This Greek-Judaic bridge John disclosed
And the Word in divine flesh enclosed:
Reason became the Word, God's will and might,
Outflowing energy, life, love and light!'

The theatre, open north-west to the bay,
Holds in embrace the sun from midday

To the last phoenix-burning on the sea:
Now, though the shade has moved some way
From the meridian when crickets doze,
The afternoon's an ember holding heat.
As for Tarragon, his scattered sparks
Fly from flint thoughts treading flinty paths:
His audience is not all captive,
Some slide from the shimmering shade away
To stroll along the Marmorean Way;
Others relax, their puckered eyes
Droop in the shower of words, content
That their subconscious may interpret it.
Some sleep. The rest observe, attentive
For some new tangential flight.

    ' "Tyger! Tyger! burning bright,"
Is much stranger in the light:
"What the hammer? What the chain?
In what furnace was the brain?" '
Simpkin whispered in my ear,
'This is where I disappear.'

Said Tarragon, 'You'ld like tit-bits of history?
'The place is rich in them. The Mermnadae
Took over Lydia, so came Croesus
Whose tale is well told by Herodotus,
Croesus, who first defeated Ephesos:
The Greeks, besieged, to save themselves from loss,
Ran ribbons to the shrine of Artemis
A mile outside the walls, and by this
Link obtained protection of the goddess.
So, when the city none-the-less
Was taken, Croesus had a greater
Temple built, the fourth, and for Her
Glory gave gold cows to Artemis
And pillars of Paeonius' artifice.

That charming intellectual soldier, Xenophon,
After the retreat of the Ten thousand, placed on
Deposit in the temple ransom
Of some captives, and when this handsome
Sum was in due course repaid,
Had a small model of the temple made
For the garden of his house at Elis,
Setting there an image of the goddess
Like the golden one but carved of cypress.
He died the year after Herostratus
Burned down the temple here in Ephesus:
Although man's lust for immortality
May be excusable obliquity,
To seek it thus was sheer iniquity.
Hardly the smoke had cleared, they set to build
The Wonder of the World, still unfulfilled
When Alexander came; Bede, in his
Work *De sept.mir.mundi* has a treatise
On its aspect that is too fantastic,
But by his time enthusiastic
Christians had claimed it as a quarry
For their churches: we may be sorry
Verde antique was taken by Justinian
For Saint Sophia, other pillars for Saint John
Theologos at Seljuk, but be not too harsh,
Since what was left was swallowed by the marsh;
Tragic it is that Ephesus was built
On a fair bay made desolate by silt.

Tragic?'

                      Tarragon was still
As a heron fishing, head thrust forward.
Centuries before these happenings,
Long before even Alexander came,
The inspiration of Ionian art

And intellect, all that was fluid
And adventurous in Greek thought,
Had fled this place. Better it were buried.
So musing, staring with rapt eyes, he said,

'Why should we make lament for Ephesus?
We do not mourn the empty case
From which the dragon-fly
Creeps, and against the sky
Spreads the transparent iridescence
Of its wings, making the heart dance,
The mind seek thought
To match such wrought
Vitality springing from dry trance,

Go! See the cornices and capitals,
The sculptured drums and pedestals,
Take sepulchral pleasure
At the dug-up treasure
Of dead streets, archaeologists delight;
Then, when eyes tire, renew your inward sight
With the ephemeral,
The true eternal,
Mind's beauty, the Greek spirit's dragon-flight.'

The listeners stirred; the acting-floor was void.

'Funny: I swear I saw him here a moment since.'
'You've been asleep. I wish I could convince
Myself he noticed me: I love,' a girl's
Laugh bubbled, 'how his hair curls
'Like a palomino's mane;
His eyes burn, but it's all in vain,
He hardly ever looks my way.'
Her friend inquired, 'Would he dare stay,
'With goddesses on watch, when play

With you might seem a blasphemy?
The Greeks took far more seriously
Than us their rituals of fertility.'
'Took, did you say, or take? Increasingly
Past-present seems to me alarmingly
All one, a state I feel disarming me.'

My love and I sit in an arbour
Of stout, truncate columns with acanthus capitals,
Where, stretched from abacus to abacus, a trellis
Is an airy bed on which vines spread diffusing
Filtered sunshine, softly shimmering
As a still sea zephyr-stirred:
The swollen grapes, heavy and pendulous,
Affront the purity of sculptured leaves.
Her brown wrist, cool on the marble,
Is entwined by loose-strung beads
Her fingers play with, blue beads bought by
Celsus' library against the evil eye:
The thick, sweet coffee tastes of rosewater,
We breathe in silence the declining day.
From the cavernous vine-shaded inn,
Voices obscure as Ionians'
Hang on our ears their intimate lives,
As unobtrusive as the lentisk bees:
We are beautifully alone and still.

Presently, when familiar voices flock,
We leave them for the white, deserted streets,
And treading their smooth sandal-silkened stones
Try to accord our sight with Tarragon's;
Not seeking him, this tacitly agreed,
We wander with no aim but what the evening
Holds of shadowed quiet hand-in-hand with love,
When all at once we come upon him, there,
Where our path opens on a little square.

94

We halt and turn. Too late! He calls to me,
    'Come quickly here and witness heresy!'

The two bend peering at a sculptured stone,
Simpkin and Tarragon, rhetoric knives
Unsheathed: Callisto is with them, watchful
Against a wall, a yaffingale arrives
To perch above her, eyeing Tarragon's
Gestures. The goddess on the pedestal
In high relief, egg-breasted, outstretched hands
Upon the heads of goats, ignores them all.

    'This figure illustrates my point, you see?
    Astonishing no one has spotted it,'
    Said Tarragon. 'They must have cleared the scree
    'Long since that covered it. Would you commit
    Yourself to say what is its period?'
Already he'd forgotten us. Simpkin replied,
    'Perhaps contemporary with Hesiod,'
    'Do you suggest this Artemis was tied
    To his theogony in Delos? Ho!
    I've got you there. You want it both ways, eh?
    Why then no vestige of her twin, Apollo?'
    'Cher collègue,' Simpkin said, 'you do betray
    Such narrowness. I merely made it clear
    At Delos what the Delians believe,
    That, after Artemis, Leto did bear
    Apollo her undoubted twin. Why grieve
    If now I seek Apollo here to prove
    Those Greeks, when Hesiod and Homer sang,
    Were justified? Your piece of treasure-trove,
    Sculptured on a pedestal, proves nothing
    To the contrary.'

                        He thrust his fingers
At the figure: Tarragon breathed hard.

'You mean to tell me no doubt lingers
When you see this Artemis! Discard
Your affectations, Simpkin; we both know
That Leto really bore one child, this Asian
Virgin, fertilising all the seed men sow
In earth or flesh, forever to maintain
The cult of mother-goddess. The Carian
Apollo had no place in Ephesos.'
Asked Simpkin, 'You ignore his cult at Klaros?'
'Indeed, no! But he went first to Crete, then Delos,
Ending up supreme at Delphi.'
'Apollo teases you,' smiled Simpkin slyly,
'Why? He is par excellence
The symbol of Greek patriarchy
When eastern matriarchy made no sense
In a progressive new society.'

The golden light pales on the pedestal,
Slowly the shadow rises to the feet
Of the great goddess; her many breasts, her hands,
Goatlings and bees glow softly in relief.
The surrounding space is flooded as a stage
Where are no half-tones, the hieratic figures
Standing there are black as the relentless shadow
Rolling upwards as the sun sinks in the seething sea;
The watching wryneck, father of Pan, has had enough,
His head cocked, and with a que - que - que
To mock the words, he swoops in undulant flight
That flicks the eye with flash of black and white,
Parting the air with whisper close as night.

Callisto speaks: her face in shadow, voice
Cool and very clear, at once precise
Yet with echo in the high vault lingering
Vibrant as a glass bowl singing.
    'You talk in clever half-truths, understanding

More than you will dare admit, fearing
The strength of some old half-forgotten thought
Which you had only half-believed was fraught
With danger to your rationality;
You call this compromise reality.'

Professor Simpkin starts, clearing his throat.
  'What's that, dear girl, do I detect a note
Of censure? Is it you don't like our style?
Or only mine?'

                    Tarragon, the while
Callisto spoke, had stood with lowered head:
Now he looks up. 'Darkness at noon,' he said.

Simpkin laughs sharply. 'What a strange cast
  'Of thought! Let's on our way; the light goes fast
With sundown. Tarragon! Are you there?'
'Yes,' comes the reply. 'I'm here. But where?'

  'Here, there,' Callisto says, 'Or a millennium hence
Are of no consequence, the tense
You live in is in presence of them all,
Compounds them all; yet you call
Out like children in the dark? But why?'

  'Because,' Simpkin complained, 'we can't decry
Our path back to the ship; you know the way.'

  'How you deceive yourself! You dare not say
That you are crying for the moon.
I am Callisto, am I not? Soon
You will see the eye of Leto's daughter
In the sky. Do you know why she brings laughter
To the male babes who cry for her?
Because their nurses brought them to the shrine

Of Artemis, moon-goddess, called divine
Mounychia at Brauron
Where the girls dance in saffron
Before marriage, and little ones as bears
Perform the ritual as Callisto's heirs;
She is the very self of Artemis
Whom you will meet in Crete as Britomartis.

I am Pelasgian from Caucasia,
Brought by Orestes and Iphigeneia
From Tauris to my new home in Attica,
Or so they say: the story of my rape by Zeus
Was a late myth-making Greek's excuse
For saying I was turned into a bear,
And so find reason for the dances where
A goat surrogate is a sacrifice.'

Cried Tarragon, 'But you omit the vice
'Of Lemnos, the girl-sacrifices there?'
'Please, please! Don't argue with her,'
Simpkin begged. 'It's grown extremely dark,
'And all this acting's gone beyond a lark.'

'The moon will soon be here.' the girl said.
'On the still air you will feel the tread
Of Eurynome dancing in nothingness;
Pelasgians were hatched from that emptiness . . .'

Emptiness . . . the word floats into the void,
Spiralling and spreading until uncoiled
In such faint prophecy of light,
As, through dawn eye-lids closed on sight,
Comes to the waking mind. Till this moment
There was but a voice: now the weak rent
In darkness shows me two heads blent
Like carvings in a black rood-screen,

Opposing Simpkin's, the carved virgin in between.

Callisto spoke like a struck lyre.
    'I have listened and tire
    Of your arrogant talk,
    How you deliberately walk
    With intellectual pride in a world of male
    Supremacy, preaching the Greeks' patriarchal
    Conquest of woman's venerated
    Primacy, in all things consecrated
    To survival of humanity,
    Without whose cosmic sanity
    Of body as of mind
    Dies all mankind.
    Are you so blind you cannot see,
    However right historically,
    There has not been, nor could be,
    Real faith in patriarchy?
    Why otherwise with such anxiety
    Insisted? Why, with Christianity,
    Did Constantine fear worship of the Virgin,
    Egyptians counter with their faith in
    Mary as the same triple goddess,
    Who in Ephesus is Artemis?
    Why did pilgrims to Saint James of Compostell'
    Wear as a symbol Aphrodite's scallop shell?
    How to Provence did the Three Marys pass,
    Magdalen, Salome, Cleophas,
    From the hill of Calvary, there
    Triad Saintes-Maries-de-la-mer?
    Your Puritans dethroned the Queen of Heaven
    And then pursued her to a coven.
    Your supremacy is haunted, a grimacing mask
    To fright away the question you must ask -
    What genius really rules the lives of men?'

A faint shadow crept across the floor. Suffusing
Light, a wave, more of a quivering
Of the blue-dark air that was not yet night,
Haloed the heads on the south-east sky; sight
Grew as the eye of Leto opened fully,
Watching the dark procession lambently.
And, as Callisto went with moon-pale face,
Tarragon trance-like followed pace by pace
On the rough stones. Simpkin held back, irresolute
To obey an unacknowledged absolute:
Then he moved too, and we after; the while,
Hands clasped, my own love wore a crescent smile.

VIII

Night voyage to Crete - A song out of Asia - Cnossos - Theseus
and Ariadne dance partridge - Dionysos intervenes - Frenzy of
Simpkin and Tarragon.

The mast-head light sways with the slow swell,
Drawing its little arc against infinity,
Moon-dimmed like the stars, receding into time:
Sometimes it seems another ship passes
With creak of strained sheet and flapping sail,
The strange-tongued song of the rowers
Filling the dark Aegean's emptiness.

Far north-east of us is Troy; Mycenae west,
And to the south our destination, Crete;
We sail the crossings of the ships
Of the Grey Minyans of Anatolia,
Hittite Luvians from Caucasus,
With man's compelling impulse for the west
In quest of some imaginable crest
Whence he can look into Elysium,
The heart of sunset,
Where Selene, sister of the sun,
Will love him as she did Endymion.

The song the sailors sing comes out of Asia,
Old a thousand years before the son of Bathsheba,
Dark epithalamium of the Eight-year king.

   'Thy body is like a palm-tree,
   Thy breasts are clusters of vine,

Let us to the vineyard early,
Thy love is better than wine,
To breathe on thy breath the apples
While buds the pomegranate;
Already the dawn grey dapples:
Beloved, be not late!'

The rhythmic, life-in-death song fades,
The black boats billowed with infinity of air
Have crossed the long path of the waning moon:
As we near Crete in the deserted darkness,
Dawn still sleeps.

This time unclaimed stretched between four and five,
When moon nor sun rules, nature is alive
In all her parts. Be the sea rough or tranquil,
It is living sea; valley, plain and hill
Speaks every one its individual voice,
The waking birds and animals rejoice
In the suspended hour when they are free
Of gods' or goddesses' supremacy:
And man, if he will keep a silent tongue,
Can look into the world when it was young
And know that what was then is eager still,
And youth not something left behind the hill.

The ship comes into pale Heraklion
Like a bird-swimmer, no wash upon
The water smoothing itself to meet
The first breath of the sun's heat.
I sink into the pool, feeling
The flood of water and light wheeling
As I rise to the fire-ball swelling
Above the mountains, and compelling
The black peaks to leave its surface,
Making their pointed shadows race

102

Homeward like bats into their caves
With flittering of little waves.
I am alone, but for gold cliffs and sea
And five millenniums watching me.

A valley runs to Cnossos from Heraklion,
Not steeply up, but with a sense of royalty
Upon a proper eminence; the plateau
There falls sharply to the east and south, to westward
Gently slopes to vineyards, cypress groves and orchards.
Over it the ruined palace spreads its web
Of myriad rooms in labyrinthine plan,
Staircases leading upward end in air
Or dive to darkness in a chthonic world.
There is a space sloping on the north-west
Beyond the palace, near the outer gate,
Where lies the theatre, rectangular,
Paved and tiered on two sides: we came here
Seeking shade while the Cretan sun's low shafts
Still lay among the trees.

                            Simpkin watched us,
Gauging his audience with wary eyes;
A little touzled still, it gave him zest
To see the people wait upon his words.

  'Here,' he declared, 'for those who've not been here
                                before,
We are on Ariadne's dancing-floor
Designed by Daedalus
Especially for the partridge-dance;
They say that Theseus
First saw her here by chance . . .
Oh, come! Don't look as though you were confused:
I know it's partly history, part myth;
But now recall. Minos was king of Crete,

                                     103

Poseidon gave to him a fine, white bull
Which sired on his wife, Pasiphae,
A monster, the bull-headed Minotaur
For which a Labyrinth was built.
Because Minos alleged Athenians
Had killed his proper son, they paid tribute
Each ninth year sev'n men and maidens
To appease the Minotaur - or dance with bulls,
Leaping their horns in dangerous, sacred sport.
Theseus, heir to the throne of Athens,
Went en tapinois as one of them
To kill the monster. Ariadne,
Minos' daughter, fell in love with him
And shewed him how to thread the labyrinth
And kill the Minotaur; you know the tale
Of how, when they'd escaped together,
Theseus deserted Ariadne,
Dionysos took her . . .'

A voice: 'And all this came from Pasiphae
'Whose lust a bull, alone, could satisfy?'

Some giggles and a deprecating cough,
Simpkin indifferently smiled them off.
    'My friends, we have not come this far
    To gloat on primitive erotica:
    This was symbolic, ritual coupling,
    A goddess-priestess with a bull-masked king;
    Minos and Minotaur may well have been one being
    Like Ariadne-Pasiphae; the killing,
    Though, in this case changed everything,
    A whole society, a way of living . . .'

    'Professor, this floor here for dancing,
    Say, what have partridges to do with it?'

104

'You'll see how the palace frescoes make it fit:
The cult at Cnossos is fertility,
Snakes symbolising immortality,
They cast their slough as moons perpetually
Wax and wane: therefore is Ariadne
Goddess of them both. The partridge dance
Is one to honour her in spring; perchance
You've seen the shameless partridges
At mating time: their hobbling encourages
Their venery. The maze their hobbling pace
Describes was used by Daedalus to trace
The Labyrinth, the way into its heart;
Labrys, the double-axe, is on the walls,
Shaped like the waxing and the waning moon,
Creative and destructive as the goddess . . .'

He stopped, an instant only, but as though he stared at death,
Then with quick words running from his held breath
Said, 'The artifacts, what you will see of pots and paintings,
Tablets of Linear A and B, are things
Of correlating value, but these last
Without the vital thread of myth held fast
Exist to some extent in vacuo;
Though not, let's say now per esempio,
When making some comparison of date
Between Mycenaean Greeks, the first late
Minoan stage, and dominant Cnossos,
Or the Egyptian-sculptured dress:
These are the gay and lovely bones,
And our presumptuous age will leave no better ones:
Yet they explain how civilised men were,
Elegantly sensitive, with arts rare
Not only for their time, who yet withal
Were frivolous - not intellectual. . .

Two thousand years B.C., Parnassos

105

Folk found kings and hieroglyphs at Cnossos,
When at the time of Egypt's Hyksos
They sailed south to the isle of Minos.
Parnassos folk? Ah, yes, Grey Minyans,
Those obscure people some call Luvians;
It's said that first to Attica they came,
Giving the first holy place its first name
In their outlandish tongue, Parnassos,
Meaning "Belonging to the temple". Whose?
We'll say serpent earth-goddess, Delphyna,
Who shares these seas with Cretan Dictynna.

Enough for now; examine on your own
What's been dismissed as myth transcribed in stone,
For here's no sieving myth from history:
The essence of all truth is mystery,
Remember that the gods know when you lie,
Especially to yourself . . .
Pretence is perilous in this precinct.'
He turned to leave, elaborately winked:
'Go now into this incandescent light,
But let no mirages betray your sight.'

I stay there while the sun burns through the trees,
Ponder the silence now the voices cease,
The others gone in little groups that peer,
Draw together, part, wave and disappear
As though the crusted earth has swallowed them.
The spread of ruins hides the great mound's shape,
A run of corridor, a staircase dives . . .
Where? To the heart-beat of the palace-shrine,
The labyrinth? All is labyrinthine.

I must be still and breathe the resined air,
Ticklish yet drowsy after the dawn watch.
Simpkin was captious as a moulting bird:

That Ephesos encounter in the dusk
Still pricked? What was the tension here at Cnossos?
Here, at the elusive seat of Minos,
A subject Simpkin cherished as his own,
He had no more than touched the dancing-floor,
One moment showed a strange anxiety,
The next, a donnish jocularity -
Then gone.
Waves of heat rise on the perimeter,
The dancing-floor's encircled by a wall
Impassable though nebulous; beyond
Is only shadow-play, inaudible . . .
The wall's stones heat my stomach where I lie,
With leaves filtering light and dappling me
To disappearence when the voices come;
My eyes dart, my tongue flickers at the song,
Silver-toned and without echo in the stillness.

'How beautiful are her feet
At the hour of the cypress' swoon,
In the dead-white silence of noon
And the still cicada heat:
How beautiful are her feet,
Who comes with subtle dancing
To will with power entrancing
The stranger who comes to Crete.
How beautiful are her feet,
Who returns when winter is gone
To bloody the royal throne,
When the birds they sing so sweet.
How beautiful is her voice,
Who rises when winter is past,
And calls on the serpent to cast
His skin, while the doves rejoice.

I lie low, a lidded lizard listening.

'Here, on this maze,
You must show me the way
Before Minos can raise
The people. I cannot stay
Longer in pretence.'

'Theseus, keep patience,
Learn how to meet the bull,
Watch and be skilful
To choose your own hour.'

'Then Ariadne, guide my power.'

'Here is my hand; my feet go before
To follow each step devised by Daedalus
On this enciphered floor,
Partridge-hobbling like his son Talus.'

'I cannot wait.'

'That,' she said gravely, 'is your fate.'

I did not move, but my eyes followed their stepping.
After a little she loosed his hand; he followed
As she swayed, hopped a pace, chasséd, then turned about,
Her upper arms lined with her shoulders, elbows bent
And hands with thumbs wide, poised clear above her hips:
Her long, flounced skirt swung solemnly and slow,
Her bodice opened to expose her breasts.
There was no moment's hesitation of control,
Each movement had precise and ancient certainty
That cast off thought or need to guide her earth-bound feet.
So, she floated; and he with quick steps pursued,
Unbalanced as a perdix gaiting, lured
By a call his ears alone embraced.
Subtly the soundless song seduced his senses,

Speeding his steps with its possessing sortilege.

No lizard on a wall, however brilliant,
Could have diverted their enraptured stare;
And I was still and mottled as the patterned stone.
At the beginning closely brushed I watched
The dancers make their labyrinthine way,
Deceptively receding to move closer,
Imperceptibly still closer to the heart.
Suddenly the susurrating skirt was silent,
The still air shimmered in suspense;
The girl wheeled and stood, an image of herself;
So sudden was her stopping, that the man crouched,
Drawing himself up slowly, breathing deep,
To meet the onset of her wild, compelling eyes;
Her bent arms straightened, right hand pointing to her feet,
The left arm raised letting a snake slip upward
On her twined wrist . . .

'Here is the heart: death and new life,' she said.
He answered her, 'The way is in my head.'

Slowly the ecstasy ebbed, drooped her painted eyes,
Her left arm lowered with the snake's head rearing,
Arched at her breasts and her body's apron,
Till with flicked finger she sent the serpent fleeing,
Released as the soul of one but lately dead.

'He is, and is not. You understand?'
'I have sworn. He shall die by this hand.'

The heavy stillness pressed me closer to the stone:
Too deep entwined to notice a rock lizard,
They pierced and threaded one another with their eyes.
Then Theseus spoke and Ariadne watched his lips,
Avid to kiss, withholding to preserve her hold.

'Now that I know
The way a partridge finds to tread
A labyrinth, I go.
They sleep as though already dead
In this heat.
They are meat
To my sword and the spears of my men
Who will come from the sea,
The bull-dancers will be free, and then,
To-night, you will leave with me.'

'But you must first hear me;
Her lips replied, else unmoving,
'It is the eve of the ninth year, and by decree
Of sun and moon Minos is ending . . .'
He bridled. 'This I know.'
'You know, but you are slow
To understand its meaning. He will not die
As a king should; his son Asterius the Minotaur
Will succeed, and that same night must lie
With the goddess; not with the people watching as before.

Do you understand?' 'I do,' he said.
'An ancient ritual I know must change
Is no concern of ours; they will be dead
To-morrow. I am here to end this strange
Decadence and beauty;
My love is not a duty.'
'But it can be so. When you have won, what then?
'Zeus will triumph, and I shall dethroned Ariadne wed.'
'So,' she said calmly, 'Cretan child-Zeus becomes your
                                                god, when
You would take a goddess to your bed.'

Vexed, he cried, 'Why riddles, when I love you
'And must go now?' 'If you wed me,' said she,

'You must know not only me, but through
What other names and forms lives Ariadne.
I can be as tender
As a dove to render
Celestial sweetness, and can be a serpent
Of the lower world.' 'Then you are womanly
'As I desire you, part earth, part firmament.
By the laden bough, I must leave instantly.'

'There is a coldness in this white-hot noon!
You swear by my image that girls hang upon a bough
And swing to fertilize, like wax and wane of moon
Or double-headed axe that hangs now
On the palace walls.
The labyrinth falls,
And what is the lot of Pasiphae and Minos?'
'Your mother and your father!' 'Mother
And not mother; father and not father. Cnossos
Is the mother-goddess' home: She! I! None other!
Where is my snake of immortality?'

For the first time he laughed. 'I can measure my length
'With anyone to victory. If you tell me
You are also Hera, I have Hercules' strength
To ravish you. He is of a Minoan tree:
Mother-husband-son,
We shall become one
As no priestess moon-cow ever was with bull-king
Masked to couple ritually beneath an oak.'
Angered, he ran from the floor: she began to sing,
Softly swaying, holding to her bare breasts his cloak.

My skin is dry and fear ripples my throat,
Leathery-gulping, pressed to the hot stone,
Compelled by the sorcerous dance and voice.
Theseus is rounding the Hall of Pillars

Where there are watchers, he skirts the guardroom
By the north-east passage; he is coming
To the turn where steps lead down to the rooms
Where great oil jars are stored in the close dark:
He is near the playroom of the children
And the queen's treasury and megaron.
The turn is narrow to the central court,
And the corridor that runs beneath it
Joins a deep bay below the Grand Staircase:
Now he . . . Aaaah!

He has stabbed the noon-drowsy guardian.

The voice persists; the cool, sweet, savage sound
Tingling my body with its waves of transference
Sways in sympathy with Theseus' swift steps,
Willing insistently his labyrinthine way.
The voice begins to slow, falling to one note
Sustained, hovering in tuneless tremolo,
A peregrine pulsating, poised
To stoop in piercing plunge.
I shrink, shrivelled,
Nerve-tortured,
Flattened,
Dry mouth quivering,
Tongue darting . . .

Silence!

The white silence of the throne-room is splashed
With blood, the bright-frescoed griffins are scarred
And the gypsum throne is filled by Theseus:
His feet spurn the body of the bull-masked
King who pants slowly . . . slower . . . to his death.

Silence!

The pillars lean, the wall beneath me moves;
I find a crevice from the windy roar
As blackness falls. Then, from the lifting dark,
The voices swell, rejoined in passion.

    'I have slain Death! The palace walls are shuddering
At Poseidon's touch; the labyrinth is down-hurled.
Come, Ariadne! My men from the sea will bring
Your women. I have changed the course of the whole
                                         world.'
    'I helped you willingly,
And love you knowingly;
So I come, Theseus, with your blood upon my lips,
Biting the mouth that feeds me as a bird its young;
Though I know what is lost going down to your ships,
The dance on the maze-floor ended, the last song sung.'

A high-flung voice suspends them, crying jeeringly,
'Go, Ariadne, knowing what will follow; take
Your moon-born lust! You, Theseus, blindly
Believe that you have harnessed her, a tide whose flow
Will always trap men's ways,
Even as she betrays
Me, cousin-husband Dionysos, goat-horned child
Of Semele, moon-self of Ariadne.
Go with your changed world, with goddess undefiled!
She will return to Crete and bear her sons by me . . .'

If they see me I can leave my tail with these three
While they stare angrily, I am laced by a tree;
Already I have shed my skin, floatingly
Rise upwards to familiar personality.

    '. . . her sons by me . . . by me . . You will agree
That it is hard to say if we can see
The truth that ever underlies these three,

Us three, one almost said, for we . . .

For we, on this dancing-floor of Cnossos,
Can use our hindsight to compare their fate
With ours,' lisped Simpkin's voice. 'Dionysos
And Theseus are but symbols of the state
Of man's split personality, his urge,
Like Theseus' to change the world through reason,
And the irrational, his need to purge
His spirit from all taint of treason
To his senses through poetic madness,
Savage joy and tragedy. Greeks knew well,
For all their talk of "nothing in excess",
Dionysos returns each spring from hell.

Theseus with Ariadne only reached,
In fact, the neighbouring isle of Naxos,
Where in the night he left his goddess beached
And sleeping, setting his sails for Delos.
Oh never trust a man of principle
Who tells his love he wants to change her life,
It means his heart is quite invincible,
No girl of spirit wants to be his wife.
Tell me, Callisto, and be fair and true,
Supposing you were faced with such a choice,
Would Theseus' patriarchy call to you
Or would you with Dionysos rejoice?'

'Such choice would not arise, nor did it then:
My wise professor, you know very well
That Ariadne in the world of men
Was partly royal, partly mystical.'
'You juggle words; but I am asking you
Who knows that Dionysos never died.
Young Theseus is contemporary too,
Who used his reason to desert his bride.'

114

'But,' Tarragon's voice rose. 'He returned,
Wed Ariadne when he'd conquered Cnossos.'
Simpkin laughed vinously, his green eyes burned:
'Ménage à trois with Dionysos.'

His arc near done, the sun directs a beam
That sets on golden fire the dancing-floor
Where the three stand, threateningly alive,
On a space where time is like a tide
Receding to dark chasms, gathering
To flow presently in waves of passion.
The shuffle of returning feet, the hum,
Make the close air more tense and tremulous,
Draw tight a circle which may leave no gap;
The outlet narrows and the waves rise, beating . . .
Then, a voice,
              'Professors, tell us more!' bleating.

The three turn: it is like the quivering sigh
Of travellers waking to a well-known world,
Part-resentful, part-relieved, bemused.
Tarragon said slowly,
             'There will be time to-night.'
He frowned as laughter splintered on his sight.
             'The vessel at Heraklion holds all of us,
           You have come far; let us go with no
                  more fuss.'

A joke, the people thought and laughed again,
But hesitating: none but the dullest
Had survived the day without anxiety,
Some sudden fear that in the labyrinth
They'd meet . . . no one could ever tell them what.
Could their professors fail them in such straits?
Such was unthinkable. A woman cried,

'We have toiled all day in the broiling sun:
We have seen shrines but nothing of a god,
Signs, though, of a very holy mother,
A virgin-goddess served by a priest-king
In a labyrinth of dark passages,
Painted walls and terrifying beauty;
In the rooms and on the stairs gaiety
Stops suddenly in the midst of laughter;
The late thunder was like a bull roaring.
We beg you to unravel this for us.'

Tarragon surveyed the panting crowd:
Simpkin should answer for his province,
Cnossos, with his knowledge unexcelled.
But dare he risk his Dionysiac power
To turn these people to a maenad throng?
His lids closed on a vision of raw flesh:
Lifting, they showed once more his calm, clear eyes.

   'Friends and companions, in recompense
   For all you have endured I shall complete
   The tale. The sea that was the one defence
   Of Crete was conquered, no mean feat,
   By Mycenaeans, who, Minoanised,
   Decided to return the compliment,
   But were, alas, not quite so civilised;
   Perhaps they burned, perhaps Poseidon sent
   An earthquake to make desolate this place
   Of decadence, bulls, beauty and priest-kings;
   Cnossos rebuilt was never as the race
   Of Minos built, whose every stone rings
   With a compelling voice.
                Meanwhile the lords
   In Mycenae went out to vanquish Troy.
   You've seen what they won there with their bronze
                         swords

Proved only a short-lived and savage joy:
The culture they had learned from the Minoans,
Applied by them to fine design in arms,
Did not preserve them from the Dorians,
Who from the outer darkness came in swarms
With unrelenting iron. The bronze age
Melted; Mycenae and Hestor's Pylos
Tiryns, Nauplia, before the dull rage
Of these barbarians all fell; Cnossos
Sank into oblivion, great darkness
Covered all the lands of Crete and Greece.'

The sweat poured off him, he had done his part;
The huddling people had grown quiet.
Callisto moved, and, as he swung around
To seek some sign from Simpkin, her black hair
Swept on his sight with the furious fume
Of the flying mane of the Mare-Headed,
Drumming his ears with galloping hooves
And high, wild cries on the moon-white mountain.

 'Simpkin! I did not mean to steal your thunder.'
The people watched him go, waiting in wonder.

When Simpkin spoke, his voice was on a leash.
  'Darkness is coming soon, sun going, moon
  Not risen; suppose to-morrow no dawn
  Peeps, and each to-morrow is the same, soon
  You'll no longer fear perpetual night, drawn
  In obscurity to live more simply,
  Casting aside your quaint, ambitious aims;
  Dulled, your imagination limply
  Droops, no reading, writing, living arts, no claims
  Upon your soul; your life is to survive.
  You do not care, your mind no longer seeks
  Creativeness from the indifferent hive.

You feel this?

                                    Thus were the Greeks,
                                    Thus might you be again
    When barbarous, vain man puts out the light;
    As Dorians with their iron, so, with rain
    Of deathly dust, to-morrow starts the flight
    Into the darkness. Yet you will carry,
    Those who survive, the same sure heritage
    Of tension as the Greeks who could marry
    Old convention with a changing stage,
    Their art and life made fluid by the stream,
    Seemingly irrelevant, subconscious,
    The vivid, free impressionistic dream
    That flowed deep from long-abandoned Cnossos.'

There is a hot gust, and a little dust
Spirals and dances on the floor
Where Simpkin stands swaying silently,
Callisto and Tarragon gone suddenly,
And the people on the perimeter shuffling,
Snuffling uneasily like herded animals
That scent a storm. Lustily, he calls to them.

    'Go to your ship, the darkness is not yet,
    And the tension creates the vision;
    Life cannot be without art,
    The blood of it is in you
    As the juice of the grapes
    In Dionysos' wreaths.
    Balance your budgets with "nothing in excess",
    But joy is in the wine-press
    Of the god who frees your spirit;
    Be one with him, virgins, and create,
    And you, men, be as gods.
    Go to your ship: Europa rides the bull
    And there are vines on his horns and in her hair;

118

The seen spurts, and you spring from the earth's loins
With the vision already in you.
Do not let it wither on the vine . . .'

The people jostle with their heads up and faint snorts:
Simpkin skips on the dancing-floor, hitching his shorts.

As sounds recede to silence, loneliness
Comes, poignant and still, to watch the cypress
Shadow on the palace hill. I sit motionless
With a hand touching me, trembling at its caress.

'Take us,' says my love, 'the foxes,
The little foxes, that spoil the vines:
For our vines have tender grapes.'

IX

Long sail to Scheria - Continuous Becoming - The nature of the
gods

It is a long sail from Heraklion to Scheria,
To the island of the Phaeacians,
With the sun setting first on the port bow
Then rising landward on the starboard beam
After the short, gibbous night
When the helmsman turns north-west
To the Ionian sea.

The moon is not yet risen nor the day quite gone
When we near Cythera. Cythera!
Between the closing lids of sea and sky
The last, intense light makes the island glow
Purple as the dye its mussels yield;
Here, where Uranus suffered horridly,
And scallop-sandalled Aphrodite
Flew from the foam with flowering, dove-filled hair,
There is no line of white,
The rocks melting in the night
As the sky shuts down
With Aphrodite and Eurynome,
Sisters of Ishatar, dancing on the sea:
Tritons conch trumpets echo the ship's bells
And catspaws on the waves scratch scallop-shells.

It is only the wind:
Timeless wind wandering in infinity.
A year with Circe, with Calypso seven,

Ten years to bring Odysseus to his home,
Stages in life or only in the mind,
Hours, years, centuries, and where?
'No Being, only a continuous Becoming',
Calls the Ionian voice from Ephesos,
Bearing the poetic spring of Pylos.

Darkness, and Pylos on the starboard beam;
A light flickers on Sphacteria,
Island of Aëdon the brown nightingale
Eternally lamenting poor Niobe,
Here, where her sole surviving grandchild reigned,
Wise Nester, Gerenian charioteer,
Tamer of horses and unrivalled counsellor . . .

'Do you think the old man is watching us,
Has he yet seen my son, Telemachus?
Up there in his palace on the hill,
Do they discuss while dining what hope still
Remains of Odysseus' returning,
Ending his continuous Becoming?'

'I doubt,' I answered tartly, 'if Telemachus
Is thinking of his father Odysseus
Just now so much as Nestor's daughter,
Polycaste, the clothes, the oil, hot water.'

'You bring me down to earth,' Tarragon said.
I did not turn my head and answered,

'It was time.'
                        Till now, too easily
I'd fallen for his game, so gracefully
Performed, I longed to ask him where he'd been
These swift, elusive hours since I had seen
His ecstasy upon the dancing floor,

121

And then his flight. What more was there in store?
But this was wholly his affair;
So in the cool, caressing air
And dolphin-dark I cleared my head.

'How comical you were,' Tarragon said.

Silence, but for the silky slapping on the ship's side
Pursuing the hushed whispering slide
Of the bow wave as we veered from shore,
Where stars were suddenly sheered off by hills or
Mountains cut jagg'd intervals in heaven.

'Has it occurred to you,' said Tarragon,
'How long it is since we passed down this coast?'

His profile was not asking me; most
Gravely he addressed the night,
Then paused for a bright brush of light
To paint the answer on the sea
In the charmed words of a phylactery.
No sign. He went on contemplatively,

'Our outward journey passed Scheria by,
Scheria, now called Corfu, the last landfall made
Before Odysseus was home. Had he stayed . . .
We passed this haunted island in the night
And then at dawn our eyes were joyed by sight
Of Ithaca. Remember that hot light
Rimming the black mountain, as the sun rose
Behind the cave divine Athene chose
For the thirteen cauldrons of Odysseus,
The golden gifts from Alcinous?
Now, with our sails set fair for home,
We break our journey's palindrome
In passing by Odysseus' Ithaca

Before we land at Scheria!

A comment on our life's predicament;
The ancient question is here evident.
Is it the quest or the quest's denouement
That the gods mean to be life fulfilment?
What sequence is there in the life you've led,
Where has your body been, and where your head?
Is it three hours, days, weeks ago your tears
Moved grim Achilles, or three thousand years?'

'Was it still earlier,' I asked suddenly,
'That you danced partridge with Callisto-Ariadne,
Or were you on the dancing-floor to-day?'

He sighed, 'All visions have originality . . .
'The everlasting problem of identity
Was for the Greeks extremely serious,
Man felt his self to be precarious
Considering how easily the gods changed shape
And with their shapes their natures, too. So, to
                                   escape
This frightening circumstance, the Greeks began
The long pursuit of "Know thyself"; each man
Must prove self-knowledge of his personality
By stretching to the limits his ability,
While holding to the "Nothing in excess"
For fear the gods should punish his hubris.'

'But heroes do defy the gods,' I said.

'Hush!' He replied. 'Men have been struck dead
For less. Would you offend the arrow
Of Apollo, or give to-morrow
To the maenads of Dionysos
Who shares the summit of Parnassos?

I

Each is a half of you, two gods inside
To tear your heart apart and bate your pride.'

'How long must we believe these things,
Figures of our imaginings?'

'Always. Only the myths will change, as we
                                        procure
New and erratic clothes cut to the new culture.
When you read Homer, Aeschylus, Euripides,
Do you feel separated by three thousand years?
Why should you? A computer's answer may,
Or may not, be more accurate than, say,
That of the Delphic Oracle whose priest
Hexameters gave in reply; at least,
The reason why the instrument is fed
Remains the same; man's mathematic dread
Yearns for answers to inform his actions
In love, war, politics or cosmic fractions.'

His hand restraining me was cold
In the hot night.

                                        'I have not told
'All that I would. I'll not be long:
We shall soon be gone like a song
Sung to the god's strung tortoise-shell,
Moon-swung by Sappho's lyric spell . . .
In Nature there is no morality,
So why expect the gods of earth and sky
To have it? They were a sublimation
Of men longing for an explanation
Of the dawn, the storm, the sprouting seed,
The burst of strength, the constant need
For succour in themselves, advice.
When praying to the gods their dice

Were loaded, men, in effect, would pray
Their higher selves to win the day:
The line that separates men from gods is nice.

Moira, your Portion, the Greeks knew transcends
The will of gods. The world spirit condescends
To all men, its impartial light
Falls on the unjust and the just. Night
Swallows man; as a leaf
Winter-laid he is replaced each spring. Grief
Does not bow Odysseus because of this,
Nor you, nor me, for we are heirs of his.
Accept the law of being but be not resigned:
That is the Greek gift to mankind.
Why should I question you? The price
You paid to make this voyage should include
Attendance at at least one sacrifice.
Your silence does not mean you think me rude?'

'Dear Tarragon, you move now through a door
Which closes on me: if my silence seems poor
Compliment, you must let in the light, for
In this darkness I can follow you no more.'

'But you will: you are far too much involved.
You have observed Callisto. May she not have
                              the key?
Odysseus' sister was so-named; but, resolved
That Achaeans had abandoned matriarchy,
Homer ignored her: she was too near to Artemis.
But I must follow, for I am impelled by my desire
To find the truth: a kind of madness.
Do you understand? As if the very fire
Of Ithaca's sunrise draws me
To the burning. But not to-morrow's dawn;
Nausicaa must first save Odysseus from the sea

125

At Scheria, before the last lap with his strength
                                        reborn.

'This is the sum of the struggle by which
The world has ever been enraged,
Herein lies the tension, the constant itch
To make, destroy and recreate that has engaged
Us always. With wordy stress
On matriarchy, patriarchal law,
Priest-king and mother-goddess,
Professors keep the ignorant in awe,
While, beneath their long noses, stalk the gods
And goddesses as they have ever done
In the protean war of man at odds
With woman. Long before Troy was won,
The West and sweet Asia, male and female
Counterparts, sun and moon deities
In whom not love nor enmity prevail,
Set pattern for all human frailties.
The endless conflict of the sexes,
The tension of whose poles creates all light,
Its passion unresolved all else eclipses
Until the world becomes hermaphrodite.'

X

Alcinous, Nausicaa and Odysseus - Simpkin's last oration - Callisto's
sublimation and Tarragon's moira - Know thyself?

An immense clarity and lassitude
Emptied the air encompassing the ship:
A Sunday quiet laid its outstretched hand
Upon the deck-bound people far from home
And stilled their murmuring: the Christian god
Had banished yesterday's affront to trust
In their commonsense and their professors:
The voice of Simpkin reassures them now,
Drowsing their ears on incalescent air.

    'It's really waste of voice to theorize
    On what Odysseus may symbolize
    With all his wanderings. You ought to know
    Without my telling to you blow by blow
    The story he himself so often told:
    How, from his leaving Troy for home, this bold
    Wanderer's voyage was vexatiously delayed;
    Though you may think the cruel gods played
    Tricks on him, it was his god-defying
    Cleverness, his arrogance and lying,
    That brought his troubles. Yet one feels his charm
    And why he should at last be saved from harm.

    He sacks Ismarus, flies the Lotus-eaters, then blinds
                        Polyphemus' eye
    And boasts of it, whereon the Cyclops' cry
    Brings certain vengeance from Poseidon

On the exultant mutilator of his son.
From then the voyage goes from bad to worse,
With spans of dalliance to ease the curse;
Odysseus' fleet, save his own ship, is smashed
By the vile Laestrygonians; next, he's washed
With the survivors on to Circe's isle
Where some are turned to swine by her, meanwhile
Hermes gives Odysseus a flower
With which to save his men and overpower
The goddess who beguiles him to her bed.

A year goes by, the crew begin to dread
They'll see their homes in Ithaca no more.
So Odysseus sets sail, drawn first to that far shore
Where the world ends, and Night contains the dead
With whom Odysseus communes. The same dread
Theme you'll find in Dante and in Milton,
Whose Hells are populous as mites in Stilton:
To say those poets pinched the notion is not fair,
Because each part that makes the Odyssey can bear
Infinite repetition, for the reason each was
Drawn from the store of earth's unconscious
Womb of myth where folk-tales also grow,
Where Noah's Ark swam on dissolving snow
Of an ice-age ending, and Jericho
Fell as seven rams horns seven times blow,
And Solomon's Shulamite is like a doe
In Crete, and Amazons . . . This overflow
Of Asia is for evermore; and so

I beg you ponder on the Odyssey,
To comprehend its immortality:
The Wanderer's trials may seem to you
Unlikely, but the thread of life is true,
His every action, like yours and mine,
Bestrides uneasily the borderline

Dividing the fulfilment from the wish.
He also has a tendency to fish
In troubled waters. Yet his compromise
With Fate we should all mirror, were we wise,
For what seems myth and strange philosophy
Is active in our mind's geography.'

Professor Simpkin gazed on the recumbent
Forms. 'Your attitudes make it incumbent
  'On me to compare you with Odysseus' crew,
  Who perished for behaving just like you
  Because their leader they ignored: inept,
  They ate the Cattle of the Sun and slept.
  Odysseus alone survived Zeus' rage:
  While living with Calypso his last stage
  Drew near which you are now approaching.
  Sleep on! But were you made, as Dante said,
  A viver come bruti? Better dead
  Than miss Odysseus with Nausicaa:
  So rest, reserve your strength for Scheria,
  The Wanderer's last haven before Ithaca.'

I cannot now recall the hour we came to Scheria,
Corcyra, the Sickle or Corfu;
Past noon it must have been, with a smooth sea,
And the sky and air a heavy lid still
Pressed closely, while in the olive groves
Through which we drove was underwater light;
Such olives grow only on Scheria,
Some tall as forest trees, climbing, stretching
From the rich soil, and wild fruit trees, apples,
Pears, pomegranates, figs and sinuous vines . . .
We left them for dark wooded mountains,
Climbing the misty heights Poseidon reared
To close the country of King Alcinous
Who crossed him by assisting Odysseus.

129

Riding above a cloudy baldachin
Suspended from the roof of heaven,
It seems the kingdom must be ever hid,
When suddenly the fabric tears and flies
And there below us is the western shore,
A tongue of land, twin harbours either side,
A sweep of curving strand with black ships beached;
Houses nearby have gardens tended well
With little streams that water tidy rows,
And near the palace vineyards where the grapes
Lie purple, drying on the warm, smooth ground.
The palace? No, I cannot see it yet,
Nor, southward of the woods, the river's mouth
Where Odysseus was cast up by the sea.

The sea now has a leaden, swollen look,
Breaking in tiny ripples that hiss white
As the teeth of a sea-beast with curled lip.
The people move down to the harbour strand
Where the white houses of Phaeacians
Sweep in a moon-sickle walled by mountains.
They sink upon the sand and close their eyes,
Whispering with sea-borrowed sibilance
Till Simpkin comes.

   'If you had been washed up like Odysseus,'
He says, 'You would have some excuse;
'But let it pass, this is the last lap
Of your journey, as of his; whatever trap
Awaits him, his endurance and panache
Bring their reward, however rash
His actions seem. See how the very firmament
Is shaken by the storm Poseidon sent!
His ship is sunk, the monstrous sea plays
With his body while he swims three days
Until he gains this river-mouth nearby.

Kissing the earth, he finds a place to lie,
'A hollow made by olives intertwined,
Where nightfall and Athene seal his mind.

Next day, Odysseus, wakened by a shriek,
And being naked and still rather weak,
Sighs, "Oh, what now? Must I be brought to bay
"By maenads coming in unmanning play
To end me after all my wanderings?"
Prepared to meet whatever Fate may bring,
A thick-leaved bough he holds before his manhood,
And thus protected sallies from the greenwood.

The screams become more piercing then . . .
But, to explain, I must return to when
King Alcinous' daughter, following her dream
Athene sent, comes to this merry stream
With all the royal clothing somewhat soiled:
This washed, her maids then bathe themselves, skins
                                                    oiled
They sing and dance, begin to play beach-ball,
The princess Nausicaa outstrips all
In beauty; when she calls the girls
To leave, one drops the ball which swiftly whirls
On the deep river, hence the girlish scream
That woke Odysseus. Striding through the stream
He faces them with bough in hand: all flee
But Nausicaa, who notes his subtle plea
Disarmingly, as fits her high position,
And his good looks despite his rough condition.
She likes especially that he compares her
To the young palm on Delos where
Apollo had been born . . .

She sees that he's no fool, her women
She recalls, rebuking them, then

Bids them bathe the stranger, oil his body,
Give him clothes and food; this prosody
Of manners Odysseus rejects
And asks them to withdraw, since he elects
To bathe himself; this done, he looks so fine
That Nausicaa, with practical design,
Tells her attendants in a clear aside
She hopes he'll stay, she'd like to be his bride;
But disappointed she is bound to be,
Since he must join his wife, Penelope.
And fitting so. Odysseus has charm, no doubt,
But one might say he's been too long about,
While Nausicaa's youth entrances us:
It has been said she wed Telemachus,
Though better writers hold, I must confess,
He married Circe, once his father's mistress:
Although to call that incest is pedantic,
I do prefer the first as more romantic.'

Simpkin consults his watch.

                                'Where's Tarragon?
 'I said I'd start this thing if he'd take on.'
No one shook off his heaviness to answer,
The waves still treacley-rollered on the shore.
 'Ah well! Odysseus, needing Nausicaa's advice
On entering her parent's palace, heeds her nice
Observations on the strict manners of the place:
Near to the town they part, Athene helps him trace
His way, disguised, to the bronze porch
And the great hall, where a gold youth holds a torch
Behind each chair arranged around the wall;
The palace guards are gold and silver dogs. All
Homer's canvas of the scene is of Minoan
Style, a word he uses is "Kyanean",
Poetic language for the deep blue of the sea;

The cool enamel tiles of lapis lazuli
Fill the whole palace with blue radiance
Where Demodocus' lyre leads youth in dance . . .
The word means also mantic, chthonic things,
But let's leave academic bandyings.

Briefly, Odysseus got all he wanted:
Nausicaa's father not only granted
Hospitality, but, when Odysseus
Had told his ageless tale, king Alcinous
Lent him a black ship that had never sailed,
With fifty-two young men who had not failed
To show such oarsmanship and courage
As would ensure a pleasant voyage -
For Odysseus - to Ithaca. This done,
The young men, I must tell, were turned to stone
By great Poseidon hunting Odysseus
Implacably for blinding Polyphemus.
You see the black rock rooted in the bay?
That was the ship, and all within it stay
As they rowed home that day . . .

                          Ah, dear colleague!' Simpkin cried,
'I've reached the point when those Phaeacians died
For guileless slighting of Poseidon's pride.'

Tarragon's kyanean eyes meet Simpkin's glance,
A wild olive branch is in his hand,
He seems puzzled at what chance
Has made him pluck it. The hot strand
Throws up the westering sun on his burned cheeks;
He stares at the sea, then to the crescent peaks.

'Those, too,' he says, 'the same god made.
Do you not feel the weight of them?
Lying there, are you not afraid

Of the high, wild ridges that hem
You all against Poseidon's element?
It is quiet now as a sleeping succubus,
But sleep yourselves, and its ardent
Passion may seduce you as was Odysseus
Trapped by Circe and Calypso and the foam.
Does all that you have witnessed seem
Unreal now that you are nearing home?
You cannot wish to find it was a dream.

But you were wondering, you want a promise
That the wanderer returns:
Not all men do, but everyman is Odysseus;
Travelling hopefully, he sometimes learns
From his ordeals, more often not,
Brave Odysseus, who seemed too witty to be caught,
Slept over-easily, whereby his lot
Became more shocking; yet he gained his port.
What he found there is quite another story;
Not everyone can transform shame to glory.

Can everyone who leaves his wife at home
Believe his own Penelope,
That she slept singly while he chose to roam
In this soul-searching, fish-swarmed sea?
Better he should. When you are dead and gone,
Whatever story they contrive
Your cuckold bones can clap to dusty scorn,
If you let nothing, when alive,
Disturb with foul suspicion any joy
You have of your Penelope.

They said Odysseus' wife submitted
To her suitors and goat-footed Pan
Was born, but this has been admitted
To be scandalous, since no man

Came across the child on Ithaca,
And Pan was worshipped long before
By shepherds of Arcadia
As Hermes' son by Dryops' daughter,
Or,' The words are luminous but low.
'Or Zeus' son when he loved Callisto.

So easily men fall in lasting error.
Do not your hearts contract with terror
At the tale Plutarch tells about Thamous,
Who heard a voice when sailing close
By here: "*Thamous, Thamous, panmegas tethnéke!*"
As the command: "Thamous, great Pan is dead;
"Go, tell the world!" But he had mistranslated
Cries from shore for All-great Tammuz, a lamenting
For Adonis, whose perpetual spring dying,
That especial dawn, was coinciding
With the cry of one declaring:'
Tarragon's voice falls, wind-whispering.
'I am the Resurrection and the Life.

Then he stands quiet with a puzzled stare,
Hearing his own words singing plangently,
Wondering, it seems, how he had come there.
'*Thamous, Thamous, panmegas tethnéke,*'
He whispers, searching the people's faces
For, it seems, one face; it is all seeming
On this shore, with the Circe'd voyagers
Watching and listening as the tideless sea
Drools and hisses and the slate sky lowers,
And vines, birds, orchards and all fruiting things
Are cockshut deeper than an evening brings.

'So,' he continues, 'was another myth created;
Such is our world, experience impregnated
And facts mated with our fantasies and fads,

135

Promiscuously as Pan coupling with Maenads.
This is the poetry of life, intemperate glory;
Ignore it, and the prose of history
Is meaningless.
Do not distress
Yourselves, accept the clear conclusion
That all you think and do springs from this fusion.'

Again he stops, his blue eyes wondering:
No sound, but a sense of far thundering,
Then a stir, and a voice clear and low,
Warm-throated:
    'It is not always so.
    Sometimes the fusion is impure,
    The vision separate and more sure.'

Callisto stands, white-armed and black-haired, on the sand,
Leaning a little backward, with one hand
Upraised as though against a pillar
Of the palace where once waited Nausicaa,
Watching Odysseus drinking with the king,
Her wide eyes shaded from the shimmering
On the dark sea by a massive roof.

    'Good fortune, Odysseus, keep you aloof
    From danger; when you reach your own country
    Remember that you owe your life to me.'

    'My life, and death in life,' Tarragon cries.
    Why do you taunt me with your sighs?
    You never could be Nausicaa,
    Since Odysseus had none of her:
    If I were truly he,
    You are Penelope:
    Here is true rationality,
    Bird-Artemis-epiphany,

Whose bear, Callisto, must my sister be . . .'

The people, roused from stupor, watching
The girl gone quickly with stride gliding,
Tarragon in two worlds, swaying:
Simpkin speaks, unanswerably calming.

   'Heureux qui comme Ulysse a fait un beau voyage,
   I can't resist the quote, while noting an *orage*
   Of a most threatening kind approaches
   To attest Poseidon's sour reproaches:
   If that's indeed the tempest's provenance,
   He's not a god with whom one takes a chance.
   So I suggest, dear friends, you follow me
   Before we're swallowed by a monstrous sea.'

They went bemused, resigned, obediently,
Grateful for being told, some mumblingly.
   'Soon,' said Tarragon, 'they will be curled
   Warm in the womb of their familiar world;
   Some may question with a new sixth sense,
   Reborn with that could make a difference.'
He stared at me, laughed, and threw back his head.
   'Why are you not with them?' he said.
   You wonder is my reason fled?
   I thank you kindly, I am wholly sane
   As man can be with self-inflicted pain,
   And that is each man's moira: to accept
   This is not to deny the true concept
   That man holds destiny in his own hands;
   Greeks without puling, broke the swaddling bands.
   Good-bye! Recall each spring a god has died,
   And ask if we deserve to be revived.'

I knew then, should we sail that night,
He would not, nor, under that light-

Destroying sky, could he find ship for Ithaca,
Callisto's home. Now pursuing her
White figure's gliding stride
He has reached her side,
When the sky's livid curtains flare
Downward in a forked tear
Of flame and a sound of ripping,
The earth groaning, the wind stripping
The vines, nothing remaining fast
But my love's hand in mine. At last
Behind us the sea's fury breaks
Its leaden seal, the flying rack makes
A white cloud, which, as the sharp light
Comes again like a fire opal, sweeps a white
Figure in a whirlwind arc up and away
Seaward with Ophion-Boreas in the spray:
Lonely Eurynome, the god's mistress,
First created, of all things creatress.

The wind passes, the hills no longer quake;
The fire ceases, and in its limpid wake
The morning and the evening star are one.